OPERA JOURNEYS LIBRETTO SERIES

Giuseppe Verdi's

OTELLO

COMPLETE LIBRETTO
with Music Highlight examples

Edited by Burton D. Fisher
Principal lecturer, *Opera Journeys Lecture Series*

Opera Journeys Publishing™ / Boca Raton, Florida

WEB SITE: www.operajourneys.com E MAIL: operaj@bellsouth.net

Otello

"Othello"

Opera in Italian in four acts

Music

by

Giuseppe Verdi

Libretto by Arrigo Boito,

after Shakespeare's tragedy

Othello, the Moor of Venice

Premiere at La Scala, Milan,

February 1887

Libretto

OTELLO

ACT I

The harbor of the island of Cyprus.
It is evening. There is a violent storm with lightning and thunder.

CIPRIOTTI:
Una vela! Una vela!
Un vessillo! Un vessillo!

CYPRIOTS:
A sail! A Sail!
A vessel! A vessel!

MONTANO:
È l'alato Leon!

MONTANO:
It's like a winged lion!

CASSIO:
Or la folgor lo svela.

CASSIO:
The lightning flashes reveal it clearly.

ALTRI CHE SOPRAGGIUNGONO:
Uno squillo!

OTHERS WHO ARRIVE:
A roar of thunder!

TUTTI:
Ha tuonato il canon!

ALL:
There's a cannon shot!

CASSIO:
È la nave del Duce.

CASSIO:
It's our leader's ship.

MONTANO:
Or s'affonda or s'inciela.

MONTANO:
The swells are sinking her.

CASSIO
Erge il rostro dall'onda.

CASSIO:
She's raising her bow over the wave.

ALCUNI CIPRIOTTI:
Nelle nubi si cela e nel mar,
e alla luce dei lampi ne appar.

SOME CYPRIOTS:
She's hiding in the clouds and the sea,
and the lightning doesn't reveal her.

TUTTI:
Lampi! tuoni! gorghi!
turbi tempestosi e fulmini!
Treman l'onde! treman l'aure!
treman basi e culmini.

ALL:
Lightning! Thunder! Whirlpools!
A tempestuous hurricane and lightning
bolts! The waves roar! The winds blast!
The seas rage!

Fende l'etra un torvo e cieco spirito di
vertigine.
Iddio scuote il cielo bieco, come un
tetro vel.
Tutto è fumo! tutto è fuoco!
L'orrida caligine si fa incendio,
poi si spegne più funesta.
Spasima l'universo, accorre a valchi
l'aquilon fantasima, i titanici oricalchi
squillano nel ciel.

Dio, fulgor della bufera!
Dio, sorriso della duna!
Salva l'arca e la bandiera
della veneta fortuna!
Tu, che reggi gli astri e il Fato!
Tu, che imperi al mondo e al ciel!
Fa che in fondo al mar placato
posi l'ancora fedel.

JAGO:
È infranto l'artimon!

RODERIGO:
Il rostro piomba su quello scoglio!

CORO:
Aita! Aita!

JAGO:
(L'alvo frenetico del mar sia la sua
tomba!)

CIPRIOTTI:
È salvo! è salvo!

VOCI INTERNE:
Gittate i palischermi!
Mano alle funi! Fermi!

CIPRIOTTI:
Forza ai remi! Alla riva!

The air is being shattered by a grim and
blind spirit.
God shakes the heavens fiercely, like a
dismal pall.
All is in smoke! All is afire!
The horrible fog is lit up,
and then extinguishes itself dismally.
The whirling of the ghastly northern
clouds are like gigantic trumpets blasts
from heaven.

God, power of the storm!
God, smile of the sands!
Save the ship and the banners that are
Venice's fortune!
You, who reign over the stars and the Fates!
You, who rule the world and heaven!
Calm the depths of the seas that the
ship may anchor safely.

IAGO:
The midsail's broken!

RODERIGO:
Her bow is plunging into that rock!

CHORUS:
Rescue him! Rescue him!

IAGO: *(to Roderigo)*
(May the furious womb of the sea be
his tomb!)

CYPRIOTS:
He is safe! He is safe!

VOICES BEHIND:
Throw the lines!
Hold the ropes! Steady!

CYPRIOTS:
Man the shore boats! To the shore!

VOCI INTERNE:
All'approdo! allo sbarco!

VOICES BEHIND:
To the landing! To the landing!

CIPRIOTTI:
Evviva! Evviva! Evviva!

CYPRIOTS:
Hail! Hail! Hail!

Maestoso
OTELLO

E - sul-ta - te! L'or - go - glio mu - sul - mano sepolto è in mar,

OTELLO:
Esultate! L'orgoglio musulmano
sepolto è in mar, nostra e del ciel è
gloria! Dopo l'armi lo vinse l'uragano.

OTHELLO: *(from the landing)*
Rejoice! The Muslim's pride is buried
in the sea. Heaven has given us glory!
After the battle we defeated the hurricane.

CIPRIOTTI:
Evviva Otello! Evviva! Evviva! Evviva!
Vittoria! Vittoria! Vittoria!
Stermino, dispersi, distrutti, sepolti
nell' orrido.

CYPRIOTS:
Hail Othello! Hail! Hail! Hail!
Victory! Victory! Victory!
Scattered, dispersed, destroyed, and
buried in the deep sea.

Avranno per *requie* la sferza dei flutti,
la ridda dei turbini, la ridda dei turbini,
l'abisso, l'abisso del mar.
Vittoria! Vittoria! Vittoria! Vittoria!

The forceful storm will be their Requiem.
The galleys of the enemy lie in the
abyss of the sea.
Victory! Victory! Victory! Victory!

Si calma la bufera.

The storm subsides.

JAGO:
Roderigo, ebben, che pensi?

IAGO: *(aside)*
Roderigo, well, what do you think?

RODERIGO:
D'affogarmi.

RODERIGO:
To drown myself.

JAGO:
Stolto è chi s'affoga per amor di donna.

IAGO:
Only a fool talks of drowning himself
for the love of a woman.

RODERIGO:
Vincer nol so.

RODERIGO:
I don't know how to succeed.

JAGO:
Su via, fa senno, aspetta
l'opra del tempo. A Desdemona bella,
che nel segreto de' tuoi sogni adori,
presto in uggia verranno i foschi baci
di quel selvaggio dalle gonfie labbra.

Buon Roderigo, amico tuo sincero
mi ti professo, nè in più forte ambascia
soccorrerti potrei.
Se un fragil voto di femmina non è
tropp'arduo nodo pel genio mio nè per
l'inferno,
giuro che quella donna sarà tua.
M'ascolta,
benchè finga d'amarlo, odio quel Moro.

IAGO:
Be sensible and wait for time to work
in your favor. The beautiful
Desdemona, whom you adore in your
secret dreams, will soon tire of the kisses
from the inflated lips of that savage.

Good Roderigo, I proclaim myself your
sincere friend, but I cannot help you in
your loftier mission.
But empty feminine vows are not
difficult for my infernal genius and
wits.
I swear that the woman will be yours.
Listen to me.
I pretend to love, but I hate that Moor.

Cassio enters and joins a group of soldiers.

E una cagion dell'ira, eccola, guarda.

Quell'azzimato capitano usurpa il
grado mio, il grado mio che in cento
ben pugnate battaglie ho meritato;
tal fu il voler d'Otello, ed io rimango
di sua Moresca Signoria, l'alfiere!

Ma, come è ver che tu Roderigo sei,
cosi è pur vero che se il Moro io fossi
vedermi non vorrei d'attorno un Jago.
Se tu m'ascolti.

It is an angry cause, listen, judge.
(pointing to Cassio)
That garishly dressed captain usurped
my rank, a rank I deserved and proved
in battle; such was Othello's wish, and
I remain an ensign to the Moor!

But, Roderigo, you know the truth.
If I was the Moor, I wouldn't want to
have an Iago around.
But you will listen to me.

(The crowd has lit a fire)

CORO:
Fuoco di gioia, l'ilare vampa
fuga la notte col suo splendor.
Guizza, sfavilla, crepita, avvampa
fulgido incendio che invade il cor.

CHORUS:
Joyous fire, whose cheerful blaze
lights the night with its splendor.
It shines, roars, crackles, rises,
and its resplendent rays fill the heart.

Dal raggio attratti vaghi sembianti	Its obscure rays move around and
movono intorno mutando stuol,	change the appearance of the crowd;
e son fanciulle dai lieti canti,	and there are young girls who sing
e son farfalle dall'igneo vol.	happy songs, and butterflies ignorant of
Arde la palma col sicomoro,	their flight. The wife and her faithful
canta la sposa col suo fedel;	husband sing of bold palms and
sull'aurea fiamma, sul lieto coro	sycamores. The happy singers sing of
soffia l'ardente spiro del ciel.	ardent love coming from Heaven.
Fuoco di gioia, rapido brilla!	Joyous fire, rapidly sparkling!
Rapido passa, fuoco d'amor!	The fire of love passes quickly!
Splende, s'oscura, palpita, oscilla,	It shines, it hides, it pulses and swings.
l'ultimo guizzo, lampeggia e muor.	In its last flickering, it trembles and dies.

The fire slowly dies. The storm has completely subsided. Iago, Roderigo,
and Cassio are grouped around a table on which there is wine.

JAGO:	**IAGO:**
Roderigo, beviam!	Roderigo, let's drink!
	(to Cassio)
Qua la tazza, Capitano.	Pass the glass, Captain.
CASSIO:	**CASSIO:**
Non bevo più.	I can't drink anymore.
JAGO:	**IAGO:** *(ready to fill Cassio's cup)*
Ingoia questo sorso.	Gulp this draught.
CASSIO:	**CASSIO:** *(moving the cup away)*
No.	No.
JAGO:	**IAGO:**
Guarda! Oggi impazza tutta Cipro!	Look! Today all Cyprus is excited!
È una notte di gioia, dunque...	It's a night of joy, so...
CASSIO:	**CASSIO:**
Cessa. Già m'arde il cervello	Stop. My head is already burning from
per un nappo vuotato.	one drink.
JAGO:	**IAGO:**
Sì, ancora bever devi.	Yes, yet you must drink again and toast
Alle nozze d'Otello e Desdemona!	the marriage of Othello and Desdemona!

CIPRIOTTI:
Evviva!

CYPRIOTS:
Hail!

CASSIO:
Essa infiora questo lido.

CASSIO: *(raises his cup and sips)*
She is the flower of these shores.

JAGO:
(Lo ascolta.)

IAGO: *(whispering to Roderigo)*
(Listen to him.)

CASSIO:
Col vago suo raggiar chiama i cuori a raccolta.

CASSIO:
She gather hearts with her charming radiance.

RODERIGO:
Pur modesta essa è tanto.

RODERIGO:
I think that she is very modest.

CASSIO:
Tu, Jago, canterai le sue lodi!

CASSIO:
You, Iago, sing her praises!

JAGO:
(Lo ascolta.)

Io non sono che un critico.

IAGO: *(softly to Roderigo)*
(Listen to him.)
(loudly to Cassio)
I am just a critic.

CASSIO:
Ed ella d'ogni lode è più bella.

CASSIO:
And she is the most beautiful of every shore.

JAGO:
(Ti guarda da quel Cassio.)

IAGO: *(aside to Roderigo)*
(Beware of that Cassio.)

RODERIGO:
Che temi?

RODERIGO:
What are you afraid of?

JAGO:
(Ei favella già con troppo bollor, la gagliarda giovinezza lo sprona, è un astuto seduttor che t'ingombra il cammino.
Bada...)

IAGO:
(He speaks with too much passion, and a hearty young woman excites him. He's a subtle seductor who obstructs your smooth path.
Be aware...)

RODERIGO:
Ebben?

RODERIGO:
Well?

JAGO:
(S'ei inebria è perduto!
Fallo ber.)

Qua, ragazzi, del vino!

IAGO:
(He's lost if he gets drunk!
Make him drink.)
(to the waiters)
Over here boys, some wine!

Iago fills glasses for himself, Roderigo, and Cassio.
With his drink in his hand, he addresses himself to Cassio and the curious crowd.

Allegro con brio

Inaffia l'ugola!
Trinca, tracanna!
Prima che svampino canto e bicchier.

Let the waters quench the thirst!
Drink and gulp it down,
before song and drink vanish.

CASSIO:
Questa del pampino verace manna
di vaghe annugola nebbie il pensier.

CASSIO: *(to Iago with cup in hand)*
This vine leaf is truly a godsend whose
divine mists cloud ones thoughts.

JAGO:
Chi all'esca ha morso del ditirambo
spavaldo e strambo beva con me! Beva
con me, beva, beva, beva con me!

IAGO:
The arrogant and impassioned one has
taken the bait, and he cannot resist its
magic. Drink with me! Drink with me!

TUTTI:
Chi all'esca ha morso.

ALL:
He has taken the bait and cannot resist.

JAGO:
(Un altro sorso è brillo egli è.)

IAGO: *(indicating the drunken Cassio)*
(One more drop and he's drunk.)

RODERIGO:
(Un altro sorso è brillo egli è.)

RODERIGO:
(One more drop and he's drunk.)

JAGO:
Il mondo palpita quand'io son brillo!
Sfido l'ironico Nume e il destin!

IAGO:
The world throbs when I am drunk!
I dare the ironic god and destiny!

CASSIO:
Come un armonico liuto oscillo;
la gioia scalpita sul mio cammin!

JAGO E CORO:
Chi all'esca ha morso.....

JAGO:
Un altro sorso e brillo egli è!

RODERIGO:
Un altro sorso e brillo egli è!

JAGO:
Fuggan dal vivido nappo i codardi!

CASSIO:
In fondo all' anima ciascun mi guardi!

JAGO:
... che in cor nascondono frodi.

CASSIO:
Non temo, non temo il ver.

JAGO:
Chi all'esca ha morso....

CASSIO:
non temo il ver....
....non temo il ver.

JAGO:
....bevi con me...

CASSIO:
non temo il ver....

JAGO:
....bevi, bevi con me.

CASSIO: *(continuing to drink)*
I'm pulsating like a harmonious lute;
happiness strikes my path.

IAGO and CHORUS::
The arrogant and impassioned one has
taken the bait....

IAGO: *(to Roderigo)*
One more drop and he's drunk!

RODERIGO: *(echoing Iago)*
One more drop and he's drunk!

IAGO:
Cowards flee this good company!

CASSIO: *(interrupting)*
Look into my soul!

IAGO:
....that is a heart hiding deceit.

CASSIO:
I have no fear, no fear of the truth.

IAGO:
The arrogant and impassioned one....

CASSIO: *(wobbly and unsteady)*
I don't fear the truth....
.....I don't fear the truth.

IAGO:
...drink with me...

CASSIO:
I don't fear the truth....

IAGO:
....drink, drink with me.

CASSIO:
....e bevo e bevo e bevo....

CIPRIOTTI:
Ah! Ah ah! Ah ah! Ah ah!

CASSIO:
Del calice....

JAGO:
(Egli è briaco fradicio.)

CASSIO:
del calice....gli orli....

JAGO:
(Ti scuoti, lo trascina a contesa.
È pronto all'ira),

CIPRIOTTI:
Ah ah! Ah ah!

JAGO:
(T'offenderà ne seguirà tumulto!)

CASSIO:
del calice....gli orli.....

JAGO:
(Pensa che puoi cosi del lieto Otello)
(turbar la prima vigilia d'amor!)

RODERIGO:
(Ed è chò che mi spinge.)

CASSIO:
....s'impor....s'impor....s'imporporino.

CIPRIOTTI:
Ah! Ah ah! Ah ah!

TUTTI:
Bevi, bevi con me, bevi con me.

CASSIO:
....and I drink and drink and drink....

CYPRIOTS: *(laughing)*
Ah! Ah ah! Ah ah! Ah ah!

CASSIO: *(cannot remember the song)*
From the chalice....

IAGO: *(to Roderigo)*
(He's dead drunk.)

CASSIO:
from the chalice....the brim....

IAGO: *(to Roderigo)*
(Go over and lure him into a fight.
His anger is up.)

CYPRIOTS: *(laughing at Cassio)*
Ah ah! Ah ah!

IAGO:
(He'll offend you and start a riot!)

CASSIO: *(resumes but suffocatingly)*
from the chalice....the brim....

IAGO:
(Think that this can disturb Othello on
his first night of love!)

RODERIGO:
(And that is what drives me.)

CASSIO:
....one blushes....blushes.

CYPRIOTS:
Ah! Ah ah! Ah ah!

ALL:
Drink, drink with me, drink with me

Montano enters and addresses Cassio.

MONTANO:
Capitano, v'attende la fazione ai baluardi.

MONTANO:
Captain, leave the party and tend your watch.

CASSIO:
Andiamo.

CASSIO: *(tottering)*
Let's go.

MONTANO:
Che vedo?

MONTANO:
What am I seeing?

JAGO:
(Ogni notte in tal guisa Cassio preludia al sonno.)

IAGO: *(to Montano)*
(Cassio is like this every night before he goes to sleep.)

MONTANO:
(Otello il sappia.)

MONTANO:
(Othello should know this.)

CASSIO:
Andiamo ai baluardi.

CASSIO:
Let's go to the watch.

RODERIGO è CIPRIOTTI:
Ah, ah! Ah, ah!

RODERIGO and CYPRIOTS:
Ah, ah! Ah, ah!

CASSIO:
Chi ride?

CASSIO:
Who laughs?

RODERIGO:
Rido d'un ebro.

RODERIGO: *(provocatively)*
I'm laughing at a drunk.

CASSIO:
Bada alle tue spalle! Furfante!

CASSIO: *(pushing Roderigo)*
Watch your back! Scoundrel!

RODERIGO:
Briaco ribaldo!

RODERIGO: *(defending himself)*
Drunken rogue!

CASSIO:
Marrano! Nessun più ti salva!

CASSIO:
Traitor! No one can save you!

MONTANO:
Frenate la mano, Signor, ve ne prego.

MONTANO: *(separating them)*
Sir, I beg you to hold your hands.

CASSIO:
Ti spacco il cerebro se qui t'interponi.

CASSIO: *(to Montano)*
I'll knock your brains out if you interrupt.

MONTANO:
Parole d'un ebro.

MONTANO:
Words from a drunk.

CASSIO:
D'un ebro?

CASSIO:
From a drunk?

The crowd draws back as Cassio and Montano draw swords.

JAGO:
(Va al porto, con quanta più possa
ti resta, gridando: sommossa! sommossa!
Va! Spargi il tumulto, l'orror. Le
campane risuonino a stormo.)

IAGO: *(aside to Roderigo)*
(Go to the port as fast as you can and
shout that there's a riot!
Go! Spread the word that there's a horrible
commotion. Ring the bells in the fortress.)

(Roderigo leaves hastily)

JAGO:
Fratelli! L'immane conflitto cessate!

IAGO:
Brothers! Stop this terrible fighting!

DONNE CIPRIOTTI:
Fuggiam!

CYPRIOT WOMEN: *(fleeing)*
Let's leave!

JAGO:
Ciel! Già gronda di sangue Montano!
Tenzon furibonda!

IAGO:
Heavens! Montano drips with blood!
What terrible fighting!

DONNE:
Fuggiam, fuggiam!

WOMEN:
Let's flee, let's flee!

JAGO:
Tregua!

IAGO:
Truce!

UOMINI:
Tregua!

MEN:
Truce!

DONNE:
S'uccidono!

WOMEN:
They're killing each other!

UOMINI:
Pace!

MEN:
Peace!

JAGO:
Nessun più raffrena quel nembo pugnace!
Sì gridi l'allarme! Satana gl'invade!

IAGO: *(to the bystanders)*
No one can stop their murderous fury!
Yes, ring the alarm! Satan possesses him!

CORO:
All'armi!! All'armi!! Soccorso! Soccorso!

CHORUS:
The alarm! The alarm! Help! Help!

Othello appears, followed by men bearing torches.

OTELLO:
Abbasso le spade!

OTHELLO:
Lower your swords!
(The fight ceases)

Olà! Che avvien? Son io fra i Saraceni?
O la turchesa rabbia è in voi trasfusa
da sbranarvi l'un l'altro?
Onesto Jago, per quell'amor che tu mi
porti, parla.

Now! What's happening? Am I among
Saracens? Have you turned into Turkish
rabble who tear one another to pieces?
If you love me, be honest Iago, and tell
me what happened.

JAGO:
Non so....qui tutti eran cortesi amici,
dianzi, e giocondi. . .ma ad un tratto,
come se un pianeta maligno avesse a
quelli smagato il senno, sguainando
l'arme s'avventano furenti, avess io
prima stroncati i pie' che qui m'addusser!

IAGO:
I don't know....a short while ago, we were
all good and merry friends. But suddenly,
like an evil star overcame their good
senses, they drew their swords and began
to battle ferociously. I would have been
the first to intervene!

OTELLO:
Cassio, come obliasti te stesso a tal
segno?

OTHELLO:
Cassio, how did you forget yourself and
your duty?

CASSIO:
Grazia...perdon....parlar non so.

CASSIO:
Thank you....pardon....I can't speak.

OTELLO:
Montano.

OTHELLO:
Montano.

MONTANO:
Son ferito.

MONTANO: *(leaning on a soldier)*
I am wounded.

OTELLO:
Ferito! Pel cielo già il sangue mio
ribolle. Ah! l'ira volge l'angelo nostro
tutelare in fuga!

Che? La mia dolce Desdemona
anch'essa per voi distolta da' suoi
sogni? Cassio, non sei più capitano.

OTHELLO:
Wounded! Heavens, my blood is
already boiling. Ah, my anger compels
me to a higher judgement.

(Desdemona appears)
What? My sweet Desdemona, you have
also had your sleep disrupted?
Cassio, you are no longer a captain.

Cassio drops his sword which Iago retrieves.

JAGO:
(Oh, mio trionfo!)

IAGO: *(to himself)*
(Oh, I am triumphant!)

OTELLO:
Jago, tu va nella città sgomenta
con quella squadra a ricompor la pace.

Si soccorra Montano.

Al proprio tetto ritorni ognun.
Io da qui non mi parto se pria non vedo
deserti gli spaldi.

OTHELLO:
Iago, go into the city, discourage any
brawling and restore peace.
(Iago leaves)
Give Montano help.
(Montano is led into the castle)
I command everybody to return home.
I shall not leave until I see that peace
has been restored.

All depart.
Othello and Desdemona remain alone.

OTELLO

Già nel - la not - te den - sa s'e - stingue ogni cla - mor,

OTELLO:
Già nella notte densa s'estingue ogni
clamor.
Già il mio cor fremebondo s'ammansa
in quest'amplesso e si rinsensa.
Tuoni la guerra e s'inabissi il mondo
se dopo l'ira immensa vien
quest'immenso amor!

OTHELLO:
The night is already full and all the
commotion has ceased.
My throbbing heart is already calmed in
your embrace.
The sounds of discord rumble, and after
the rage, such a vast love overcomes it!

DESDEMONA:

Mio superbo guerrier! Quanti tormenti,
quanti mesti sospiri e quanta speme
ci condusse ai soavi abbracciamenti!
Oh! com'è dolce il mormorare insieme:
te ne rammenti!

Quando narravi l'esule tua vita
e i fieri eventi e i lunghi tuoi dolor,
ed io t'udia coll'anima rapita
in quei spaventi e coll'estasi in cor.

OTELLO:

Pingea dell'armi il fremito, la pugna
e il vol gagliardo alla breccia mortal,
l'assalto, orribil edera, coll'ugna
al baluardo e il sibilante stral.

DESDEMONA:

Poi mi guidavi ai fulgidi deserti,
all'arse arene, al tuo materno suol;
narravi allor gli spasimi sofferti
e le catene e dello schiavo il duol.

OTELLO:

Ingentilia di lagrime la storia
il tuo bel viso e il labbro di sospir;
scendean sulle mie tenebre la gloria,
il paradiso e gli astri a benedir.

DESDEMONA:

Ed io vedea fra le tue tempie oscure
splender del genio l'eterea beltà.

DESDEMONA:

My proud warrior! How much agony and
torment, how many sorrows and hopes
have brought you to these gentle embraces!
Oh! You remember well our sweet
whispers together.!

When you told me of the terrible events in
your life, the long suffering and your
exile, my enraptured soul heard those
frights with ecstasy.

OTHELLO:

I told you about the battles, trembling
fears, the prowess in crushing mortals,
the assault, the horrible accidents, and
the flood of impending death.

DESDEMONA:

Then you guided me to the resplendent
deserts, the scorched fields, to the mother's
soil, and you told me again of the pains you
suffered as a slave in chains.

OTHELLO:

The history evoked gentle tears on your
face, and your lips sighed.
The glory of paradise and the star's
blessings descended from them.

DESDEMONA:

And I saw shining between your dark
temples, the splendor of genius and the
beauty of your spirit.

OTELLO

E   tu m'amavi per le mie sventure   ed io t'a - mavo per la tua   pie-tà.

OTELLO:
E tu m'amavi per le mie sventure
ed io t'amavo per la tua pietà.

OTHELLO:
And you loved me for the dangers I had
passed and I loved you that you did pity them.

DESDEMONA:
Ed io t'amavo per le tue sventure
e tu m'amavi per la mia pietà.

DESDEMONA:
And I loved you for the dangers you had
passed and you loved me that I did pity them.

OTELLO:
E tu m'amavi....

OTHELLO:
And you loved me....

DESDEMONA:
E tu m'amavi....

DESDEMONA:
And you loved me....

OTELLO:
Ed io t'amavo...

OTHELLO:
And I loved you....

OTELLO, DESDEMONA:
....per la {tua, mia} pietà!

OTHELLO, DESDEMONA:
....for (your, my) pity!

OTELLO:
Venga la morte! E mi colga nell'estasi
di quest'amplesso il momento
supremo!

OTHELLO:
Let death come! I find myself in the
ecstasy of this embrace, this supreme
moment!

The sky is clear: the stars shine, and the moon rises.

Tale è il gaudio dell'anima che temo,
temo che più non mi sara concesso
quest'attimo divino nell'ignoto avvenir
del mio destino.

It is the joy of the soul that I fear.
I fear that in my unknown destiny,
I will no longer be comforted by such a
divine moment.

DESDEMONA:
Disperda il ciel gli affanni e amor non
muti col mutar degli anni.

DESDEMONA:
Let the heavens disperse grief, and may
our love never change as the years pass.

OTELLO:
A questa tua preghiera *Amen* risponda
la celeste schiera.

OTHELLO:
The celestial voices respond *Amen* to
your prayer.

DESDEMONA:
Amen risponda.

DESDEMONA:
They answer *Amen.*

OTELLO:
Ah! La gioia m'innonda si fieramente,
.che ansante mi giacio.
Un bacio.

OTHELLO:
Ah! I am filled with joy. Yes, I
surrender my pride.
A kiss.

DESDEMONA:
Otello!

DESDEMONA:
Othello!

Allegro moderato

OTELLO:
Un bacio....ancora un bacio.

Già la pleiade ardente al mar discende.

OTHELLO:
A kiss....another kiss.
(looking skyward)
The burning Pleiades are already
descending into the sea.

DESDEMONA:
Tarda e la notte.

DESDEMONA:
It is late in the night.

OTELLO:
Vien. Venere splende.

OTHELLO:
Come. Venus shines brightly.

DESDEMONA:
Otello!

DESDEMONA:
Othello!

Embraced, Othello and Desdemona enter the castle.

ACT II

A Hall in the Castle. A terrace and a large garden are in the background.

JAGO:
Non ti crucciar. Se credi a me, tra poco
farai ritorno ai folleggianti amori
di Monna Bianca, altiero capitano,
coll'elsa d'oro e col balteo fregiato.

IAGO:
Don't worry, proud captain. If you
listen to me, soon you will adorn your
golden sword and return to the joyful
love of Monna Bianca.

CASSIO:
Non lusingarmi.

CASSIO:
Don't deceive me.

JAGO:
Attendi a ciò ch'io dico.
Tu dei saper che Desdemona è il Duce
del nostro Duce, sol per essa ei vive.
Pregala tu, quell'anima cortese
per te interceda e il tuo perdono è certo.

IAGO:
Listen to what I say.
You must know that Desdemona
overwhelms our leader, and he only lives for
her. Plead with her, and that genteel soul will
intercede for you, and your pardon is certain.

CASSIO:
Ma come favellarle?

CASSIO:
But how can I talk to her?

JAGO:
È suo costume girsene a meriggiar fra
quelle fronde colla consorte mia. Qui vi
l'aspetta. Or t'è aperta la via di
salvazione. Vanne.

IAGO:
At noon it is her custom to rest among
the arbors with my wife. You can await
her here. I have unveiled the path to
your salvation. Go.
(Cassio leaves)

JAGO:
Vanne; la tua meta già vedo.
Ti spinge il tuo dimone,
e il tuo dimon son io.

IAGO: *(following Cassio with his eyes)*
Go. I already see your fate.
Your demon drives you, and I am that
demon.

E me trascina il mio, nel quale io credo,
inesorato Iddio.

And mine drives me to my faith in a
relentless god.

Allegro sostenuto

Credo in un Dio crduel che m'ha creato simile a se e che nell'ira io nomo.	I believe in a cruel god who has created me in his image, and I call upon in my wrath.

Dalla viltà d'un germe o d'un atomo vile son nato. Son scellerato perchè son uomo, e sento il fango originario in me. Sì! questa è la mia fè!	I was born from a vile germ or a vile atom. I am wicked because I am human, and I feel the slime of the genesis within me. Yes! That is my faith!

Credo con fermo cuor, siccome crede la vedovella al tempio, che il mal ch'io penso e che da me procede, per il mio destino adempio.	I strongly believe, like a young widow before the altar, that the evil I think, and the evil that flows from me, is the fulfillment of my destiny.

Credo che il giusto è un istrion beffardo, e nel viso e nel cuor, che tutto è in lui bugiardo: lagrima, bacio, sguardo, sacrificio ed onor.	I believe that justice is a pretence that mocks the mind and heart, those deceptive tears, kisses, prayers, glances, sacrifice and honor.

E credo l'uom gioco d'iniqua sorte dal germe della culla al verme dell'avel.	And I believe humanity receives an iniquitous fate, from the worm of the cradle to the worm of the death.

Vien dopo tanta irrision la Morte. E poi? E poi? La Morte è' il Nulla. È vecchia fola il Ciel.	After all this senselessness comes death. And then? And then? Death is nothingness. Heaven is an old fable.

Desdemona and Emilia appear in the garden. Iago directs Cassio to them.

JAGO:	**IAGO:**
Eccola....Cassio....a te....questo è il momento. Ti scuoti....vien Desdemona.	Cassio, there she is. This is the moment for you. Hurry. Desdemona is coming.

Cassio approaches Desdemona in the garden, bows and joins her.

S'è mosso; la saluta e s'avvicina. Or qui si tragga Otello! Aiuta, aiuta Satana il mio cimento! Già conversano insieme, ed essa inclina, sorridendo, il bel viso.	He approaches her. He greets her, and he joins her. Now I must fetch Othello! Satan help me, help my experiment succeed! They're already talking together, and she tilts her beautiful smiling face.

Cassio and Desdemona pass back and forth as they converse in the garden.

Mi basta un lampo sol di quel sorriso	All I need is a flash of that smile to
per trascinare Otello alla ruina.	drag Othello to his ruin.

Iago goes rapidly toward the door but suddenly stops.

Andiam. Ma il caso in mio favor	To work. All my endeavors are working
s'adopra.	for me. *(Othello enters)*
Eccolo. Al posto, all'opra.	Her he is. To my post. To work.

Iago stares intently toward the garden and talks to himself,
pretending not to see Othello entering.

JAGO:
Ciò m'accora.

IAGO:
That breaks my heart.

OTELLO:
Che parli?

OTHELLO:
What are you saying?

JAGO:
Nulla. Voi qui? Una vana voce m'uscì
dal labbro.

IAGO:
Nothing. You here? An idle word
escaped from my lips.

OTELLO:
Colui che s'allontana dalla mia sposa, è
Cassio?

OTHELLO:
Who is that person over there with my
wife? Is it Cassio?

JAGO:
Cassio? No, quei si scosse come un reo
nel vedervi.

IAGO:
Cassio? No. He would flee like a
criminal if he would see you.

OTELLO:
Credo che Cassio ei fosse.

OTHELLO:
I believe I saw Cassio.

JAGO:
Mio signore.

IAGO:
My lord.

OTELLO:
Che brami?

OTHELLO:
What is your desire?

JAGO:
Cassio, nei primi dì del vostro amor,
Desdemona non conosceva?

IAGO:
Did Desdemona know Cassio when you
were first courting her?

OTELLO:
Sì. Perchè fai tale inchiesta?

OTHELLO:
Yes, but why do you ask?

JAGO:
Il mio pensiero è vago d'ubbie, non di
malizia.

IAGO:
My thoughts are without prejudice and
without malice.

OTELLO:
Di' il tuo pensiero, Jago.

OTHELLO:
Iago, speak you thoughts.

JAGO:
Vi confidaste a Cassio?

IAGO:
Have you confided to Cassio?

OTELLO:
Spesso un mio dono o un cenno
portava alla mia sposa.

OTHELLO:
He would often bring my gifts or a
message to my wife.

JAGO:
Dassenno?

IAGO:
Really?

OTELLO:
Sì, dassenno.
Nol credi onesto?

OTHELLO:
Yes, really.
You don't believe he is honest?

JAGO:
Onesto?

IAGO:
Honest?

OTELLO:
Che ascondi nel tuo core?

OTHELLO:
What are you hiding in your heart?

JAGO:
Che ascondo in cor, signore?

IAGO:
My lord, what do I hide in my heart?

OTELLO:
"Che ascondo in cor, signore?"
Pel cielo, tu sei l'eco dei detti miei, nel
chiostro dell'anima ricetti qualche
terribil mostro.

OTHELLO:
"Lord, what do I hide in my heart?"
For heavens sake, you're echoing my
very words. In the refuge of your soul
you are hiding some terrible thoughts.

Sì, ben t'udii poc'anzi mormorar: "Ciò
m'accora."
Ma di che t'accoravi?
Nomini Cassio e allora tu corrughi la
fronte.
Suvvia, parla, se m'ami.

Yes, I indeed heard you mumbling
before: "That breaks my heart."
But what was upsetting you?
You invoke the name of Cassio, and
then you wrinkle your brow.
Come now, if you love me, speak to me.

JAGO:
Voi sapete ch'io v'amo.

IAGO:
You know that I love you.

OTELLO:
Dunque senza velami t'esprimi, e senza
ambagi.
T'esca fuor dalla gola il tuo più rio
pensiero colla più ria parola.

OTHELLO:
Then reveal yourself and express
yourself without ambiguity and mystery.
Speak your most wicked thought and
most wicked word.

JAGO:
S'anco teneste in mano tutta l'anima
mia nol sapreste.

IAGO:
If you would hold my soul in your hand
you wouldn't know.

OTELLO:
Ah!

OTHELLO:
Ah!

JAGO:
Temete, signor, la gelosia!

IAGO: *(whispering to Othello)*
My lord, do you fear jealousy?

Moderato
IAGO

È   un'i - dra   fos   -   ca,   li - vi - da,

È un'idra fosca, livida, cieca, col suo
veleno sè stessa attosca, vivida piaga le
squarcia il seno.

It is a green-eyed monster, dark, livid,
and blind. It poisons itself, rips open its
own wounds, and feeds on them.

OTELLO
Miseria mia! No! Il vano sospettar nulla
giova.
Pria del dubbio l'indagine, dopo il
dubbio la prova, dopo la prova (Otello
ha sue leggi supreme), amore e gelosia
vadan dispersi insieme!

OTHELLO:
Misery! No! Nothing will help this vain
suspect.
Before doubt, comes investigation, and
after doubt, the proof (Othello has his
own supreme rules), and then love and
jealousy will disappear together!

JAGO:
Un tal proposto spezza di mie labbra il suggello.

Non parlo ancor di prova, pur, generoso Otello, vigilate. Soventi le oneste e ben create coscienze non vedono la frode: vigilate.
Scrutate le parole di Desdemona, un detto può ricondur la fede, può affermare il sospetto.

IAGO:
Your proposal unseals my lips.

Don't speak more of proof, generous Othello. Be vigilant, for often honest people with good conscience do not see the deceit of others. Watch.
Scrutinize Desdemona's words. A mere word can restore faith, or it can affirm suspicions.

In the garden, Desdemona is surrounded by women, children, and Cypriot and Albanian sailors. All offer her flowers, gifts, and sing her praises.

VOCI LONTANO:
Dove guardi splendono
raggi, avvampan cuori,
dove passi scendono
nuvole di fiori.
Qui fra gigli e rose,
come a un casto altare,
padri, bimbi, spose
vengono a cantar.

VOICES FROM AFAR:
The sun shines
where you fix your eyes.
Where you walk, hearts inflame, and
new flowers descend.
Here among the chaste altar of lilies
and roses,
fathers, children, and spouses come to
sing as if it is a chaste altar.

JAGO:
Eccola....vigilate.

IAGO:
Here she is. Scrutinize her.

FANCIULLI:
T'offriamo il giglio soave stel
che in man degl' angeli fu assunto in
ciel, che abbella il fulgido manto
e la gonna della Madonna
e il santo vel.

CHILDREN: *(spreading lilies)*
We offer you slender-stemmed lilies
that the angels have taken from heaven,
that adorn the sparkling mantle, the
Madonna's dress,
and the sainted veil.

DONNE E MARINAI:
Mentre all' aura vola
lieta la canzon,
l'agile mandola
ne accompagna il suon.

WOMEN AND SAILORS:
While the happy song floats with the
breeze,
the sprightly mandolin
accompanies the song.

Sailors give Desdemona necklaces of corals and pearls.

MARINAI:
A te le porpore, le perle e gli ostri,
nella voragine colti del mar.
Vogliam Desdemona coi doni nostri
come un'immagine sacra adornar.

SAILORS:
We offer you pearls and corals,
gathered from the depths of the sea.
We want our gifts to adorn Desdemona
like a sacred image.

DONNE E FANCIULLI:
Mentre all' aura vola
lieta la canzon,
l'agile mandola
ne accompagna il suon.

WOMEN AND CHILDREN:
How happy the song floats with the
breeze,
the sprightly mandolin
accompanies the song.

LE DONNE:
A te la florida messe dai grembi
spargiam al suolo, a nembi, a nembi.
L'april circonda la sposa bionda
d'un etra rorida che vibra al sol.

WOMEN: *(spreading flowers)*
In your honor we spread harvests of
flowers to the ground like clouds.
April encircles the blond wife with a
moist dew that quivers in the sun.

FANCIULLI E MARINAI
Mentre all' aura vola....

CHILDREN AND SAILORS:
While the breezes blow...

TUTTI:
Dove guardi splendono raggi...

ALL:
Where you see splendid rays....

DESDEMONA:
Splende il cielo, danza l'aura, olezza il
fior.

DESDEMONA:
The sky shines, the breezes dance, the
flowers are fragrant.

OTELLO:
Quel canto mi conquide.
S'ella m'inganna, il ciel se stesso
irride!

OTHELLO:
That song conquers me.
If she is deceiving me, heaven itself has
been scorned!

JAGO:
(Beltà ed amor in dolce inno concordi!
I vostri infrangerò soavi accordi.)

IAGO:
(Beauty and love are in gentle harmony! I
will break these gentle accords.)

DESDEMONA:
Gioia, amor, speranza cantan nel mio cor.

DESDEMONA:
Joy, love and hope sing in my heart.

CIPRIOTTI:
Vivi felice! Vivi felice!
Addio. Qui regna Amor.

CYPRIOTS:
Live happily! Live happily!
Farewell. Here love reigns.

OTELLO:
Quel canto mi conquide.

OTHELLO:
That song has conquered me.

Desdemona leaves the admirers and enters the hall with Emilia.

DESDEMONA

D'un uom che geme,   sotto il tuo disde - gno   la preghie - ra   ti porto.

DESDEMONA:
D'un uom che geme sotto il tuo
disdegno la preghiera ti porto.

DESDEMONA: *(to Othello)*
I bring you a prayer from a man who
laments because of your disdain.

OTELLO:
Chi è costui?

OTHELLO:
Who would he be?

DESDEMONA:
Cassio.

DESDEMONA:
Cassio.

OTELLO:
Era lui che ti parlava sotto quelle
fronde?

OTHELLO:
Was it Cassio who was speaking to you
under those fronds?

DESDEMONA:
Lui stesso, e il suo dolor che in me
s'infonde tanto è verace che di grazia è
degno. Intercedo per lui, per lui ti
prego. Tu gli perdona.

DESDEMONA:
None other. I feel his pain so deep within
me. He is so truthful and deserves mercy. I
am interceding with you on his behalf.
You must forgive him.

OTELLO:
Non ora.

OTHELLO: *(sternly)*
Not now.

DESDEMONA:
Non oppormi il tuo diniego.
Gli perdona.

DESDEMONA:
Don't oppose me with your denial.
Forgive him.

OTELLO:
Non ora.

OTHELLO:
Not now.

DESDEMONA:
Perchè torbida suona la voce tua?
Qual pena t'addolora?

DESDEMONA:
Why is your voice so troubled?
What pain afflicts you?

OTELLO:
M'ardon le tempie.

OTHELLO:
My forehead is on fire.

DESDEMONA:

Quell'ardor molesto svanirà, se con
questo morbido lino la mia man ti fascia.

DESDEMONA: *(about to apply the
handkerchief to Othello's forehead)*
I'll bind this soft cloth, and that
annoying heat will vanish.

OTELLO:

Non ho d'uopo di ciò.

OTHELLO: *(throwing the
handkerchief to the ground)*
I have no need for it.

DESDEMONA:
Tu sei crucciato, signor.

DESDEMONA:
You are upset, my lord.

OTELLO:
Mi lascia! Mi lascia!

OTHELLO: *(roughly)*
Leave me alone! Leave me alone!

(Emilia picks up the handkerchief)

DESDEMONA:
Se inconscia, contro te, sposo, ho
peccato, dammi la dolce e lieta parola
del perdono.

DESDEMONA:
My husband, if I have unconsciously
sinned against you, give me the sweet
and blessed word of your forgiveness.

Largo
DESDEMONA

Dam - mi la dol - ce e lie - ta paro - la del per - donno.

OTELLO:
(Forse perchè gl'inganni
d'arguto amor non tendo...)

OTHELLO: *(aside)*
(Perhaps because I am not deceitful and
pretend ardent love...)

DESDEMONA:
La tua fanciulla io sono umile e
mansueta; ma il labbro tuo sospira,
hai l'occhio fiso al soul.

Guardami in volto e mira come favella
amor.
Vien ch'io t'allieti il core, ch'io ti
lenisca il duol.
Guardami in volto e mira....

OTELLO:
(....forse perchè discendo nella valle
degli anni, forse perchè ho sul viso
quest'atro tenebror....
forse perchè gl'inganni d'arguto
amor non tendo.

Ella è perduta e irriso io sono e il core
m'infrango e ruinar nel fango vedo il
mio sogno d'or.
Ella è perduta e irriso.

JAGO:
(Quel vel mi porgi ch'or hai raccolto.)

EMILIA:
(Qual frode scorgi?
Ti leggo in volto.)

JAGO:
(T'opponi a voto quand'io commando.)

EMILIA:
(Il tuo nefando livor m'è noto.)

JAGO:
(Sospetto insano!)

EMILIA:
(Guardia fedel è questa mano.)

DESDEMONA:
I am your little girl, humble and meek.
But your lips bear sighs, and your eyes
are transfixed to the ground.

Look in my face and see how it speaks
of love.
Come let me enliven your heart, and
soothe your pain.
Look in my face....

OTHELLO:
(....perhaps because I am getting older,
or perhaps because my face bears a
darkness....
perhaps because I mistake the sincerity
of the love she offers me.

She is lost and I am mocked.
My heart broken and I see my golden
dream ruined in slime.
She is lost and I am mocked.

IAGO: *(aside to Emilia)*
(Give me that veil you just picked up.)

EMILIA:
(What hoaxes are you hatching?
I read it in your face.)

IAGO:
(I am in command, and I oppose your
refusals.)

EMILIA:
(I know too well the wicked side of you.)

IAGO:
(Insane suspicions!)

EMILIA:
(This hand is faithful.)

JAGO:
(Dammi quel vel!
Su te l'irosa mia man s'aggrava!)

IAGO: *(with violence)*
(Give me that veil!
My angry hand will strike you!)

EMILIA:
(Son la tua sposa, non la tua schiava.)

EMILIA:
(I am your wife, not your slave.)

JAGO:
(La schiava impura tu sei di Jago.)

IAGO:
(You are Iago's impure slave.)

EMILIA:
(Ho il cor presago d'una sventura.)

EMILIA:
(I feel omens of misfortune in my heart.)

JAGO:
(Nè mi paventi?)

IAGO:
(You don't fear me?)

EMILIA:
(Uomo crudel!)

EMILIA:
(Cruel man!)

JAGO:
(A me.)

IAGO:
(Give it to me.)

EMILIA:
(Che tenti?)

EMILIA:
(What are you attempting?)

JAGO:
(A me quel vel!)

IAGO:
(Give me that veil!)

(Iago tears the handkerchief from Emilia)

EMILIA:
(Uomo crudel!)

EMILIA:
(Cruel man!)

JAGO:
(Già la mia brama conquido, ed ora
su questa trama Jago lavora!)

IAGO: *(to himself)*
(I got what I wanted. Now Iago will
develop his plot!)

EMILIA:
(Vinser gli artigli truci e codardi.
Dio dai perigli sempre ci guardi.)

EMILIA: *(to herself)*
(His cruel and cowardly claws won.
God save us always against perils.)

DESDEMONA:
Dammi la dolce e lieta parola del perdon.

DESDEMONA:
Give me the sweet and joyful word of your forgiveness.

OTELLO:
Escite! Solo vo' restar.

OTHELLO:
Leave me! I want to be alone.

JAGO:
(Ti giova tacer. Intendi?)

IAGO: *(whispering to Emilia)*
(You should remain quiet! (Do you understand?)

(Desdemona and Emilia exit)

OTELLO:
Desdemona rea!

OTHELLO: *(exhausted, falls into a chair)*
Desdemona is guilty!

JAGO:
(Con questi fili tramerò la prova del peccato d'amor. Nella dimora di Cassio ciò s'asconda.)

IAGO: *(looking at the handkerchief)*
(With these threads I will plot the proof of sinful love. I will hide this in Cassio's house.)

OTELLO:
Atroce idea!

OTHELLO:
An atrocious idea!

JAGO:
(Il mio velen lavora.)

IAGO: *(watching Othello)*
(My poison is working.)

OTELLO:
Rea contro me! contro me!

OTHELLO:
Guilty against me! Against me!

JAGO:
(Soffri e ruggi!)

IAGO:
(Suffer and scream!)

OTELLO:
Atroce! Atroce!

OTHELLO:
Atrocious! Atrocious!

JAGO:
Non pensateci più.

IAGO:
Don't think about it any more.

(approaches Othello cordially)

OTELLO:
Tu? Indietro! Fuggi!

OTHELLO: *(staggering)*
You? Get back! Flee from here!

M'hai legato alla croce! Ahimè!
Più orrendo d'ogni orrenda inguiria
dell' ingiuria è il sospetto.

You have tied me to the cross! Alas!
Suspicion is the most horrible of the
most horrible of injustices.

Nell' ore arcane della sua lussuria
(e a me furate!) m'agitava il petto forse
un presagio?

During the mysterious hours of lust
stolen from me (and it infuriates me!)
was I being agitated by this omen?

Ero baldo, giulivo.
Nulla sapevo ancora; io non sentivo sul
suo corpo divin che m'innamora e sui
labbri mendaci gli ardenti baci di Cassio!

I was bold, joyful.
Yet I knew nothing. On her lying lips
and divine body that enamored me, I
didn't feel Cassio's ardent kisses!

Ed ora! ed ora!

And now! And now!

Allegro assai sostenuto
OTELLO

O - ra e per sempre   ad - dio   san - te   me - morie,

Ora e per sempre addio sante memorie,
addio, sublimi incanti del pensier!

Now and forever farewell to noble
memories, farewell to sublime,
enchanted thoughts!

Addio schiere fulgenti,
addio vittorie, dardi volanti e volanti
corsier!
Addio, vessillo trionfale e pio,
e diane squillanti in sul mattin!
Clamori e canti di battaglia, addio!
Della gloria d'Otello è questo il fin.

Farewell to resplendent echelons,
farewell to victories, to flying missiles
and the flying corsair!
Farewell to the triumphant, pious vessel,
and the blaring morning reveille!
Farewell to the clamors and songs of
battle! The is the end of Othello's glory.

JAGO:
Pace, signor.

IAGO:
Peace, my lord.

OTELLO:
Sciagurato! Mi trova una prova secura
che Desdemona è impura.
Non sfuggir! Nulla ti giova!
Vo' una secura, una visibil prova!
O sulla tua testa s'accenda e precipiti il
fulmine del mio spaventoso furor che si
desta!

OTHELLO:
Wretched one! Find me certain proof
that Desdemona is impure.
Do not escape! Nothing will help you!
I want sure, visible proof!
Or I will ignite and awaken the
lightning of my frightening rage on
your head!

Othello grasps Iago by his throat and throws him down.

JAGO:
Divina grazia difendimi!
Il cielo vi protegga. Non son più vostro
alfiere.
Voglio che il mondo testimon mi sia
che l'onestà è periglio.

IAGO:
Defend me merciful heaven!
May Heaven protect you! I am no
longer your ensign.
I want the world to be my witness that
it has been perilous for me to be honest.

(Iago pretends to leave)

OTELLO:
No...rimani. Forse onesto tu sei.

OTHELLO:
No. Stay. Perhaps you are honest.

JAGO:
Meglio varebbe ch'io fossi un
ciurmador.

IAGO: *(still pretending to withdraw)*
Perhaps it would have been wise for me
to be a swindler.

OTELLO:
Per l'universo!
Credo leale Desdemona e credo
che non lo sia.

Te credo onesto e credo
disleale.
La prova io voglio!
Voglio la certezza!

OTHELLO:
For the sake of humanity!
I believe Desdemona is loyal and I
believe that she is not.

I believe that you are honest and I
believe that you are disloyal.
I want proof!
I want certainty!

JAGO:
Signor, frenate l'ansie.
E qual certezza v'abbisogna?
Avvinti verderli forse?

IAGO: *(returning to Othello)*
My lord, curb your anxiety.
And what certainty do you need?
Perhaps you want to see them embraced?

OTELLO:
Ah, morte e dannazione!

OTHELLO:
Ah, death and damnation!

JAGO:
Ardua impresa sarebbe; e qual certezza
sognate voi se quell' immondo fatto sempre
vi sfuggirà? Ma pur se guida è la ragione al
vero, una si forte congettura riserbo che per
poco alla certezza vi conduce. Udite.

IAGO:
It would truly be difficult. And what
certainty do you dream of if that filthy
deed eludes you? But even if truth is
guided by reason, use strong judgment
to lead you to certainty. Listen!

Era la notte, Cassio dormia, gli stavo
accanto.
Con interrotte voci tradia l'intimo
incanto.
Le labbra lente, lente movea, nell'
abbandono del sogno ardente, e allor
dicea, con flebil suono:

It was night. Cassio was sleeping, and I
stayed close to him.
With a broken voice he revealed his
most intimate enchantments.
His lips moved very slowly, and in the
abandonment of his ardent dream,
he then said:

"Desdemona soave! Il nostro amor
s'asconda. Cauti vegliamo! L'estasi del
ciel tutto m'innonda."

"Gentle Desdemona! Hide our love. We
must be cautious! Heaven's ecstasy
completely enraptures me."

Seguia più vago l'incubo blando;
con molle angoscia l'interna imago
quasi baciando, ei disse poscia:

His gentle nightmare became more
indistinct, and while almost kissing the
dreamy image, he said with anguish:

"Il rio destino impreco che al Moro ti
donò."
E allora il sogno in cieco letargo si
mutò.

"I curse the awful destiny that gave you
to the Moor."
And then the dream became silent
slumber.

OTELLO:
Oh! Mostruosa colpa!

OTHELLO:
Oh! Monstrous guilt!

JAGO:
Io non narrai che un sogno.

IAGO:
I only related a dream.

OTELLO:
Un sogno che rivela un fatto.

OTHELLO:
A dream that reveals the truth.

JAGO:
Un sogno che può dar forma di prova
ad altro indizio.

IAGO:
A dream that can provide proof of
something else.

OTELLO:
E qual?

OTHELLO:
And what?

JAGO:
Talor vedeste in mano di Desdemona
un tessuto trapunto a fior e più sottil
d'un velo?

IAGO:
Have you ever seen Desdemona
holding a fine veil, a cloth embroidered
with flowers?

OTELLO:
È il fazzoletto ch'io le diedi, pegno
primo d'amor.

OTHELLO:
It is the handkerchief that I gave her as
the first pledge of my love.

JAGO:
Quel fazzoletto ieri lo vidi in man di
Cassio.

IAGO:
I saw that handkerchief yesterday in
Cassio's hands.

OTELLO:
Ah! Mille vite gli donassse Iddio!
Una è povera preda al furor mio!
Jago, ho il cor di gelo.
Lungi da me le pietose larve!
Tutto il mio vano amor esalo al cielo,
guardami, ei sparve.
Nelle sue spire d'angue l'idra m'avvince!
Ah! Sangue! Sangue! Sangue!

OTHELLO:
Ah! May God give him a thousand lives!
His prayers are too weak for my furor!
Iago, I have a heart of ice.
Keep the miserable larva away from me!
All my vain love has risen to heaven.
Look at me. The Hydra has me trapped
in its bloody coils!
Ah! Blood! Blood! Blood!

Molto Sostenuto

Si, pel ciel marmoreo giuro!
Per le attorte folgori!
Per la Morte e per l'oscuro mar sterminator!
D'ira e d'impeto tremendo presto fia
che sfolgori questa man ch'io levo e stendo!

Yes, I swear by the marble heaven!
By the twisted lightning above!
By death and the obscure annihilating sea!
This hand I extend in anger and wrath
shall avenge me!

JAGO:
Non v'alzate ancor!
Testimon è il Sol ch'io miro,
che m'irradia e inanima l'ampia terra e
il vasto spiro del Creato inter,
che ad Otello io sacro ardenti, core,
braccio ed anima s'anco ad opere
cruenti s'armi il suo voler!

IAGO:
Do not rise yet!
I witness it, by the sun I see,
that illuminates me and breathes life to
the vast earth from the Creator's breath.
I give my heart and soul to Othello's
sacred passion, fastened to his bloody
commands, and braced to his wishes!

Together, they raise their hands in a solemn oath.

JAGO è OTELLO:
Sì, pel ciel marmoreo giuro!
Per le attorte folgori!
Per la Morte e per l'oscuro mar sterminator!
D'ira e d'impeto tremendo presto fia
che sfolgori questa man ch'io levo e stendo!
Dio vendicator!

IAGO and OTHELLO:
Yes, I swear by the marble heaven!
By the twisted lightning above!
By death and the obscure, annihilating sea!
This hand I extend in anger and wrath
shall avenge me!
God will vindicate us!

ACT III

The Great Hall of the Castle. Othello converses with Iago.

ARALDO:
La vedetta del porto ha segnalato
la veneta galea che a Cipro adduce
gli ambasciatori.

HERALD:
The watch at the port has signaled that
a Venetian galley has come to Cyprus
with the ambassadors.

OTELLO:
Bene sta.

Continua.

OTHELLO:
It is well.
(to Iago)
Continue.

JAGO:
Qui trarrò Cassio e con astute inchieste
lo adescherò a ciarlar.
Voi là nascosto scrutate i modi suoi, le
sue parole, i lazzi, i gesti.
Paziente siate o la prova vi sfugge.

Ecco Desdemona.
Finger conviene. Io vado.
Il fazzoletto.....

IAGO:
I'll draw Cassio here, and with astute
questions, I'll lure him to speak.
You will hide there and scrutinize his
manners, his words, his gibes, his gestures.
You must be patient or the proof will escape.

Here comes Desdemona.
It is best to pretend to be proper.. I am going.
The handkerchief.....

OTELLO:
Va! Volentieri obliato l'avrei.

OTHELLO:
Go! I would have gladly forgotten it.

Allegro moderato
DESDEMONA

Dio ti gicondi o spo - so,   dell'alma mi- a sov -ra   -   no.

DESDEMONA:
Dio ti giocondi, o sposo dell'alma mia sovrano.

DESDEMONA:
God bring joy to my husband, the master over my soul.

OTELLO:
Grazie, madonna, datemi la vostra eburnea mano. Caldo mador ne irrora la morbida beltà.

OTHELLO:
Thank you my good lady., Give me your ivory hand, whose mellow beauty is sprinkled with warmth.

DESDEMONA:
Essa ancor l'orme ignora del duolo e dell'età.

DESDEMONA:
It yet is ignorant of the marks of age or sorrow.

OTELLO:
Eppur qui annida il demone gentil del mal consiglio, che il vago avorio allumina del piccioletto artiglio. Mollemente alla prece s'atteggia e al pio fervore.

OTHELLO:
And here nestles the gentle demon of evil advice, which illuminates the vague ivory of this hand.
It requires one to softly pose in prayer and pure ardor.

DESDEMONA:
Eppur con questa mano io v'ho donato il core.

DESDEMONA:
And yet it was with this hand that I have given you my heart.

Ma riparlar vi debbo di Cassio.

But I must speak to you again of Cassio.

OTELLO
Ancor l'ambascia del mio morbo m'assale; tu la fronte mi fascia.

OTHELLO:
Again the anguish of my disease assaults me; bandage my forehead.

DESDEMONA:
A te.

DESDEMONA: *(offering a handkerchief)*
Here.

OTELLO:
No; il fazzoletto voglio ch'io ti donai.

DESDEMONA:
Non l'ho meco.

OTELLO:
Desdemona, guai se lo perdi! Guai!
Una possente maga ne ordia lo stame
arcano.
Ivi è riposta l'alta malia d'un
talismano.
Bada! Smarrirlo, oppur donarlo, è ria
sventura!

DESDEMONA:
Il vero parli?

OTELLO:
Il vero parlo.

DESDEMONA:
Mi fai paura!

OTELLO:
Che? L'hai perduto forse?

DESDEMONA:
No.

OTELLO:
Lo cerca.

DESDEMONA:
Fra poco lo cercherò.

OTELLO:
No, tosto!

DESDEMONA:
Tu di me ti fai gioco storni cosi
l'inchiesta di Cassio; astuzia è questa
del tuo pensier.

OTHELLO:
No, I want the handkerchief I gave you
as a present.

DESDEMONA:
I don't have it with me.

OTHELLO:
Desdemona, woe if you lost it! Woe!
A powerful sorceress was plotting the
mysterious thread.
The powerful spell of an evil talisman
is hidden here.
Enough! Losing it or giving it away
would be a bad misfortune!

DESDEMONA:
Really?

OTHELLO:
Yes, it is true.

DESDEMONA:
You scare me!

OTHELLO:
What? Perhaps you lost it?

DESDEMONA:
No.

OTHELLO:
Look for it.

DESDEMONA:
I'll look for it later.

OTHELLO:
No, right away.

DESDEMONA:
Your making fun of me. In this way
you're evading my inquiry about Cassio.
Your thoughts are cunning.

OTELLO:
Pel cielo! L'anima mia si desta!
Il fazzoletto.

OTHELLO:
By heavens! My soul awakens!
The handkerchief.

DESDEMONA:
È Cassio l'amico tuo diletto.

DESDEMONA:
Cassio is your favorite friend.

OTELLO:
Il fazzoletto!

OTHELLO:
The handkerchief!

DESDEMONA
A Cassio, a Cassio perdona.

DESDEMONA:
Forgive Cassio.

OTELLO:
Il fazzoletto!

OTHELLO:
The handkerchief!

DESDEMONA:
Gran Dio! Nella tua voce v'è un grido
di minaccia!

DESDEMONA:
Good God! The shouting of your voice
is menacing!

OTELLO:
Alza quegli occhi!

OTHELLO:
Lift those eyes!

DESDEMONA:
Atroce idea!

DESDEMONA:
Horrible idea!

Othello physically forces Desdemona to look at him.

OTELLO:
Guardami in faccia! Dimmi chi sei!

OTHELLO:
Look into my face! Tell me who you are!

DESDEMONA:
La sposa fedel d'Otello

DESDEMONA:
The faithful wife of Othello.

OTELLO:
Giura! Giura e ti danna.

OTHELLO:
Swear it! Swear it and damn yourself.

DESDEMONA:
Otello fedel mi crede.

DESDEMONA:
Othello, believe me, I am faithful.

OTELLO:
Impura ti credo.

OTHELLO:
I believe you are unfaithful.

DESDEMONA:
Iddio m'aiuta!

DESDEMONA:
God help me!

OTELLO:
Corri alla tua condanna, di' che sei casta.

OTHELLO:
Go to your damnation, and say you are chaste.

DESDEMONA:
Casta io son.

DESDEMONA:
I am chaste.

OTELLO:
Giura e ti danna!

OTHELLO:
Swear it and damn yourself!

DESDEMONA:
Esterre fatta fisso lo sguardo tuo tremendo, in te parla una Furia, la sento e non l'intendo.

DESDEMONA:
I am terrified by your look. A fury speaks inside you. I feel it but cannot understand it.

Mi guarda! il volto e l'anima ti svelo; il core infranto mi scruta. Io prego il cielo per te con questo pianto, per te con queste stille cocenti aspergo il suol.

Look at me! I reveal my face and soul to you. My heart is broken. I search inside myself. In tears I pray to heaven for you, sprinkling my scalding tears on the ground.

Guarda le prime lagrime, che da me spreme il duol.

Look at my tears, that have been caused by my pain.

OTELLO:
S'or ti scorge il tuo demone, un angelo ti crede e non t'afferra.

OTHELLO:
Perhaps it perceives your demon. An angel may believe you but not grasp it.

DESDEMONA:
Vede l'Eterno la mia fede!

DESDEMONA:
God is aware of my faithfulness!

OTELLO:
No! La vede l'inferno.

OTHELLO:
No! Hell sees it.

DESDEMONA:
La tua giustizia impetro, sposo mio!

DESDEMONA:
My husband, I implore your justice!

OTELLO:
Ah! Desdemona! Indietro! Indietro! Indietro!

OTHELLO:
Ah! Desdemona! Back! Back! Back!

DESDEMONA:
Tu pur piangi? E gemendo freni del cor
lo schianto!
E son io l'innocente cagion di tanto pianto!
Qual è il mio fallo?

DESDEMONA:
Are you crying also? And by moaning
you stop your pain!
And I am the innocent cause of your tears!
What have I done wrong?

OTELLO:
E il chiedi? Il più nero delitto sovra il
candido giglio della tua fronte è scritto.

OTHELLO:
And you ask? The darkest sin is written
on the whiteness of your forehead.

DESDEMONA:
Ahimè!

DESDEMONA:
Oh my!

OTELLO:
Che? Non sei forse una vil cortigiana?

OTHELLO:
What? Are you not perhaps a vile courtesan?

DESDEMONA:
Ciel! No, no, pel battesmo della fede
cristiana!

DESDEMONA:
Heaven! No, no, by the baptism of my
Christian faith!

OTELLO:
Che?

OTHELLO:
What?

DESDEMONA:
Ah! Non son ciò che esprime quella
parola orrenda.

DESDEMONA:
Ah! I am not what you say, that horrible
word.

Othello changes from wrath to calm irony.
He takes Desdemona's hand and leads her to the door.

OTELLO:
Datemi ancor l'eburnea mano, vo' fare
ammenda.
Vi credea (perdonate se il mio pensiero
è fello) quella vil cortigiana che è la
sposa d'Otello.

OTHELLO:
Give me again your ivory hand, I want
to apologize.
I believe (please forgive me if my
thoughts are treacherous) that Othello's
wife is a vile courtesan.

Othello pushes Desdemona out.
He becomes deeply dejected, his voice suffocating.

Dio! Mi potevi scagliar tutti i mali
della miseria, della vergogna,
far de' miei baldi trofei trionfali
una maceria, una menzogna.

E avrei portato la croce crudel
d'angoscie e d'onte con calma fronte
e rassegnato al volere del ciel.

Ma, o pianto, o duol! M'han rapito il
miraggio dov'io, giulivo, l'anima
acqueto.

Spento è quel sol, quel sorriso, quel
raggio che mi fa vivo, che mi fa lieto!
Tu alfin, Clemenza, pio genio
immortal dal roseo riso,
copri il tuo viso santo coll'orrida larva
infernal!

Ah! Dannazione!
Pria confessi il delitto e poscia muoia!
Confession! Confession!
La prova!

God! You could have afflicted me with
all the pains of poverty and shame.
From my bold triumphs you have given
me ruination and lies.

And I would have borne the cruel cross
of anguish and dishonor calmly and with
resignation if it was the wish of Heaven.

But, oh tears, oh pain! They have
robbed me of the illusion of joy and
calm in my soul.

The sun has descended, that smile, that
radiance that gave me life and joy!
You at least, clemency, pious immortal
genius of a rosy smile,
cover your sainted face with the
horrible infernal larva!

Ah! Damnation!
First confess the crime and then you die!
Confession! Confession!
Proof!

(Iago enters)

JAGO:
Cassio è là!

IAGO:
Cassio is there!

OTELLO:
Là? Cielo! Oh, gioia!

OTHELLO:
There? Heavens! Oh, joy!

Orror! Supplizi immondi!

Horror! Filthy torments!

JAGO:
Ti frena! Ti nascondi!

IAGO: *(leads Othello to the back)*
Stop! Hide yourself!

JAGO:
Vieni, l'aula è deserta.
T'inoltra, o Capitano.

(Iago meets Cassio)
Come, the hall is deserted.
Come forward, Captain.

CASSIO:
Questo nome d'onor suona ancor vano
per me.

CASSIO:
The honorable title still sounds vain to
me.

JAGO:
Fa cor, la tua causa è in tal mano che la
vittoria è certa.

IAGO:
Take heart, your cause is in such good
hands that victory is certain.

CASSIO:
Io qui credea di ritrovar Desdemona.

CASSIO:
I thought that I would find Desdemona here.

OTELLO:
Ei la nomò!

OTHELLO: *(from hiding)*
He named her!

CASSIO:
Vorrei parlarle ancora, per saper se la
mia grazia è profferta.

CASSIO:
I want to speak to her again to know if
my pardon has been granted.

JAGO:
L'attendi.

IAGO:
Await her.

Iago leads Cassio near to where Othello hides so he can overhear them.

E intanto, giacche non si stanca mai la
tua lingua nelle fole gaie, narrami un
po' di lei che t'innamora.

Meanwhile, don't let your tongue tire,
and tell about your cheerful adventures.
Tell a little about the one who loves you.

CASSIO:
Di chi?

CASSIO:
Who?

JAGO:
Di Bianca.

IAGO: *(whispering to Cassio)*
Of Bianca.

OTELLO:
(Sorride!)

OTHELLO:
(He laughs!)

CASSIO:
Baie!

CASSIO:
Nonsense!

JAGO:
Essa t'avvince coi vaghi rai.

IAGO:
She conquers you with her charming glow.

CASSIO:
Rider mi fai.

CASSIO:
You make me laugh.

JAGO:
Ride chi vince.

IAGO:
The victor laughs.

CASSIO:
In tai difide, per verità, vince chi ride.
Ah! Ah!

CASSIO:
In such challenges, truly, the victor
laughs. Ah! Ah!

JAGO:
Ah! Ah!

IAGO:
Ah! Ah!

OTELLO:
(L'empio trionfa, il suo scherno m'uccide.
Dio frena l'ansia che in core mi sta!)

OTHELLO:
(Impious triumph! His scorn kills me.
God restrain the anxiety in my heart!)

CASSIO:
Son già di baci sazio e di lai. O amor
fugaci!

CASSIO:
I've already had enough of kisses and
fleeting love!

JAGO:
Rider mi fai!

IAGO:
You make me laugh!

Vagheggi il regno d'altra beltà.
Colgo nel segno? Ah! Ah!

Some other beauty has enchanted you.
Did I catch you? Ah! Ah!

CASSIO:
Ah! Ah!

CASSIO:
Ah! Ah!

OTELLO:
(L'empio m'irride, il suo scherno m'uccide,
Dio frena l'ansia che in core mista!)

OTHELLO:
(Impious triumph! His scorn kills me.
God restrain the anxiety in my heart!)

CASSIO:
Nel segno hai coto. Si, lo confesso.
M'odi.

CASSIO:
You have hit the mark. Yes, I confess
it. Listen to me.

JAGO:
Sommesso parla. T'ascolto.

IAGO:
Speak softly. I'm listening to you.

Iago leads Cassio far from where Othello can hear.

CASSIO:
Jago, t'è nota la mia dimora.

CASSIO:
Iago, you know my apartment.

OTELLO:
(Or gli racconta il modo, il luogo e l'ora.)

OTHELLO:
(Now he's telling him the way, place, and the hour.

CASSIO:
Da mano ignota....

CASSIO:
From some unknown hand....

OTELLO:
(Le parole non odo....
Lasso! e udir le vorrei! Dove son guinto!)

OTHELLO:
(I can't hear your words....
I want to hear them! Look where I wait!)

CASSIO:
....un vel trapunto....

CASSIO:
....a veil with three point design....

JAGO:
È strano! È strano!

IAGO:
That's strange! That's strange!

OTELLO:
(D'avvicinarmi Jago mi fa cenno.)

OTHELLO:
(Iago makes a sign for me to get closer.)

JAGO:
Da ignota mano?
Baie!

IAGO:
From an unknown hand?
Nonsense!

CASSIO:
Da senno.
Quanto mi tarda saper chi sia.

CASSIO:
Really.
I can't figure out who it is.

JAGO:
(Otello spia.)

L'hai teco?

IAGO: *(looking toward Othello)*
(Othello is spying.)
(to Cassio, loudly)
You have it with you?

CASSIO:
Guarda.

CASSIO: *(taking out the handkerchief)*
Look.

JAGO:
Qual meraviglia!

IAGO: *(taking the handkerchief)*
What a wonder!

(Otello origlia. Ei s'avvicina con mosse accorte.)

(Othello listens. He comes closer cautiously..)
(to Cassio)

Bel cavaliere.

Handsome cavalier.
(Iago holds the handkerchief behind him for Othello to see)

Nel vostro ostello perdono gli angeli l'aureola e il vel.

In your home angels lose their veils and their wings..

OTELLO:

OTHELLO:
(looking at the handkerchief)

(È quello! È quello!)
Ruina e morte!

(That is it! That is it!
Death and ruin!

JAGO:
(Origlia Otello.)

IAGO: *(to himself)*
(Othello listens.)

OTELLO:
(Tutto è spento! Amore e duol.
L'alma mia nessun più smuova.)

OTHELLO: *(whispering)*
(All is ended! Love and pain.
Nobody move my soul anymore.)

Allegro brillante
IAGO

Quest è una ra - gna dove il tuo cuor casca, si lagna, s'impiglia e muor.

JAGO:
Questa è una ragna
dove il tuo cuor
casca, si lagna,
s'impiglia e muor.
Troppo l'ammiri,
troppo la guardi;
bada ai deliri
vani e bugiardi.
Questa è una ragna....

IAGO: *(displaying the handkerchief)*
This is a web
where your heart
falls, moans,
becomes entangled and dies.
You admire her
and look at her so much.
Be aware of useless
and false illusions.
This is a web....

CASSIO:
Miracolo vago dell'aspro e dell'ago
che in raggi tramuta le fila d'un vel,
più bianco, più leve che fiocco di neve,
che nube tessuta dalla'aure del ciel.

CASSIO:
Charming miracle of the reel and needle
that transform the threads into a glimmering
veil, whiter and lighter than flakes of snow,
like a cloud woven by breezes in the sky.

JAGO:
Questa è una ragna dove il tuo cuor....

IAGO:
This is a web where your heart....

CASSIO:
Miracolo vago....

CASSIO:
Miraculous charm....

OTELLO:

(Tradimento, tradimento, tradimento,
la tua prova, la tua prova spaventosa
mostri al Sol.)

OTHELLO: *(Hidden and looking at the handkerchief in Cassio's hands)*
(Treachery, treachery, treachery,
your proof, your proof, frightening
lights of the sun.)

CASSIO:
Miracolo vago!

CASSIO:
Charming miracle!

OTELLO:
(Tradimento!)

OTHELLO:
(Treachery!)

JAGO:
Troppo l'ammiri....

IAGO: *(to Cassio)*
You admire her....

OTELLO:
(Tradimento!)

OTHELLO:
(Treachery!)

Trumpets and canon sound from afar.

JAGO:
Bada! Bada!

IAGO:
Listen! Listen!

Quest'è il segnale che annuncia
l'approdo della trireme veneziana.
Ascolta.
Tutto il castel co'suoi squilli risponde.
Se qui non vuoi con Otello scontrarti,
fuggi.

This is the signal that announces the
arrival of the Venetian galley.
Listen.
The whole castle blasts its response.
If you don't want to face Othello here,
then run away.

CASSIO:
Addio.

CASSIO:
Farewell.

JAGO:
Va.

IAGO:
Go.

As Cassio leaves, Othello emerges from hiding.

OTELLO:
Come la ucciderò?

OTHELLO:
How shall I kill her?

JAGO:
Vedeste ben com'egli ha riso?

IAGO:
You saw well how he laughed?

OTELLO:
Vidi.

OTHELLO:
I saw.

JAGO:
E il fazzoletto?

IAGO:
And the handkerchief?

OTELLO:
Tutto vidi.

OTHELLO:
I saw all.

CIPRIOTTI:
Evviva! Alla riva!

CYPRIOTS:
Hail! To the shore!

VOCI LONTANE:
Allo sbarco!

VOICE FROM AFAR:
To the landing!

OTELLO:
È condannata.

OTHELLO:
She is condemned.

TUTTI:
Evviva!

ALL:
Hail!

OTELLO:
Fa ch'io m'abbia un velen per questa notte.

OTHELLO:
Get me some poison for this evening.

JAGO:
Il tosco, no.

IAGO:
Poison. No!

TUTTI:
Evviva il Leon di San Marco!

ALL:
Hail the Lion of St. Marks!

JAGO:
Val meglio soffocarla, là nel suo letto,
là, dove ha peccato.

IAGO:
Much better to suffocate her in her bed
where she has sinned.

OTELLO:
Questa giustizia tua mi pace.

OTHELLO:
Your sense of justice pleases me.

JAGO:
A Cassio Jago provvederà.

IAGO:
Iago will handle Cassio.

OTELLO:
Jago, fin d'ora mio Capitano t'eleggo.

OTHELLO:
Iago, from this moment I elect you my Captain.

JAGO:
Mio Duce, grazie vi rendo.
Ecco gli Ambasciatori.
Li accogliete. Ma ad evitar sospetti,
Desdemona si mostri a quei Messeri.

IAGO:
My leader, I give you thanks.
Here are the Ambassadors.
Receive them. But avoid suspicion and present Desdemona to those gentlemen.

OTELLO:
Si, qui l'adduci.

OTHELLO:
Yes, bring her here.

Iago leaves. Othello goes to greet the Ambassadors. All gather: Iago, Lodovico, Roderigo, the Herald, Desdemona and Emilia, Dignitaries of the Venetian Republic, Gentlemen, ladies, and soldiers.

TUTTI:
Viva! Evviva!
Viva il Leon di San Marco.
Evviva, evviva!

ALL:
Long life! Hail!
Hail to the Lion of St. Marks.
Hail, hail!

LODOVICO:
Il Doge ed il Senato salutano l'eroe trionfatore di Cipro. Io reco nelle vostre mani il messaggio dogale.

LODOVICO: *(holding a parchment)*
The Doge and the Senate salute the triumphant hero of Cyprus. I deliver to your hands the Doge's message.

OTELLO:
Io bacio il segno della Sovrana Maestà.

OTHELLO: *(takes the letter and kisses it)*
I kiss the seal of the Sovereign Majesty.

(Othello opens the letter and reads it)

LODOVICO:
Madonna, v'abbia il ciel in sua guardia.

LODOVICO: *(going to Desdemona)*
My lady, may heaven protect you.

DESDEMONA:
E il ciel v'ascolti.

DESDEMONA:
May heaven hear you.

EMILIA:
(Come sei mesta!)

DESDEMONA:
(Emilia, una gran nube turba il senno
d'Otello e il mio destino.)

JAGO:
Messere, son lieto di vedervi.

LODOVICO:
Jago, quali nuove? Ma in mezzo a voi
non trovo Cassio.

JAGO:
Con lui crucciato è Otello.

DESDEMONA:
Credo che in grazia tornerà.

OTELLO:
Ne siete certa?

DESDEMONA:
Che dite?

LODOVICO:
Ei legge, non vi parla.

JAGO:
Forse che in grazia tornerà.

DESDEMONA:
Jago, lo spero; sai se un verace affetto
io porti a Cassio.

OTELLO:
Frenate dunque le labbra loquaci. . .

DESDEMONA:
Perdonate, signor.

EMILIA: *(aside to Desdemona)*
(How sad you are!)

DESDEMONA: *(aside to Emilia)*
(Emilia, a heavy cloud is upsetting
Othello's mind and my destiny.)

IAGO: *(to Lodovico)*
Sirs, I'm happy to see you.

LODOVICO:
Iago, what is new? I don't see Cassio
among you.

IAGO:
Othello is upset with him.

DESDEMONA:
I believe he will return to his good graces.

OTHELLO: *(to Desdemona)*
Are you so sure?

DESDEMONA:
What are you saying?

LODOVICO:
He's reading, and doesn't speak to you.

IAGO:
Perhaps his kindness will return.

DESDEMONA:
Iago, I hope so. You know how much
true affection I have for Cassio.

OTHELLO: *(whispering to Desdemona)*
Hold your babbling tongue.

DESDEMONA:
Pardon me, my lord.

OTELLO:
Demonio, taci!

OTHELLO: *(about to strike Desdemona)*
Damn it, quiet!

LODOVICO:
Ferma!

LODOVICO: *(holding back Othello)*
Stop!

TUTTI:
Orrore! Orrore!

ALL:
Horror! Horror!

LODOVICO:
La mente mia non osa pensar ch'io vidi
il vero.

LODOVICO:
My mind doesn't dare to think that I
saw such a deed.

OTELLO:
A me Cassio!

OTHELLO: *(commanding the Herald)*
Bring Cassio to me!

JAGO:
(Che tenti?)

IAGO: *(whispering to Othello)*
What are you doing?

OTELLO:
(Guardala mentre ei giunge.)

OTHELLO: *(aside to Iago)*
(Watch her when he arrives.)

GENTILUOMINI:
Ah! Triste sposa!

MEN:
Ah! Sad wife!

LODOVICO:
Quest'è dunque l'erore? quest'è il
guerriero dai sublimi ardimenti?

LODOVICO: *(aside to Iago)*
Is this the hero? Is this the warrior with
sublime boldness?

JAGO:
È quel ch'egli è.

IAGO:
He is the one.

LODOVICO:
Palesa il tuo pensiero.

LODOVICO:
Reveal your thoughts.

JAGO:
Meglio è tener su ciò la lingua muta.

IAGO:
It is better not to talk about it.

OTELLO:
(Eccolo! È lui!
Nell'animo lo scruta.)

OTHELLO: *(to Iago, as Cassio appears)*
(Here he comes! It's him!
Watch him carefully.)

Messeri! Il Doge....

(ben tu fingi il pianto.)
mi richiama a Venezia.

RODERIGO:
(Infida sorte!)

OTELLO:
E in Cipro elegge mio successor colui
che stava accanto al mio vessillo,
Cassio.

JAGO:
(Inferno e morte!)

OTELLO:
La parola Ducale è nostra legge.

CASSIO:
Obbedirò.

OTELLO:
(Vedi? Non par che esulti l'infame!)

JAGO:
(No.)

OTELLO:
La ciurma e la coorte....

(Continua i tuoi singulti)
e le navi e il castello lascio in poter del
nuovo Duce.

LODOVICO:
Otello, per pietà la conforta o il cor le
infrangi.

OTELLO:
Noi salperem domani.

Gentlemen! The Doge....
(aside to Desdemona)
(you pretend your tears well)
has recalled me to Venice.

RODERIGO:
(Deceitful fate!)

OTHELLO:
And elects as my successor in Cyprus,
the man who stood beside me on my
vessel: Cassio.

IAGO: *(surprised and furious)*
(Hell and death!)

OTHELLO:
The Ducal word is our law.

CASSIO: *(bowing to Othello)*
I will obey.

OTHELLO: *(to Iago)*
(Look? It seems the villain is not excited!)

IAGO:
(No.)

OTHELLO:
The crew and the court...
(aside to Desdemona)
(Continue your weeping)
and the ships and the castle are left
under the command of the new leader.

LODOVICO: *(pointing to Desdemona)*
Othello, for pity's sake, comfort her or
you will break her heart.

OTHELLO: *(to Lodovico and Desdemona)*
We sail tomorrow.

Othello grabs Desdemona furiously and throws her to the ground..
Emilia and Lodovico lift her and try to comfort her.

A terra! E piangi!   To the ground! And weep!

Largo
DESDEMONA

DESDEMONA: DESDEMONA:
A terra! Si, nel livido fango, percossa,   On the ground! Yes, in the murky mud.
.io giacio, piango, m'agghiaccia il   Struck down, I lie weeping, the shiver
brivido dell'anima che muor.   of my chills in my dying soul.

E un di sul mio sorriso   And once my smile flourished with
fioria la speme e il bacio,   hope and a kiss,
ed or, l'angoscia in viso   and now, there is anguish on my face
e l'agonia nel cor.   and agony in my heart.

Quel Sol sereno e vivido   That serene and vivid sun that enlivens
che allieta il cielo e il mare   the heavens and the sea
non può asciugar le amare   cannot ease the bitterness
stille del mio dolor.   of my pain.

EMILIA   EMILIA:
(Quell 'innocente un fremito   (That innocent shudders from his hate.
d'odio non ha nè un gesto,   Deep in her bosom the sigh dies, wrung
trattiene in petto il gemito   by her grief. She restrains the painful
con doloroso fren.   moaning in her heart.
La lagrima si frange muta sul volto mesto;   The tears fall silent on her sad face.
no, chi per lei non piange non ha   No. The one who cannot weep for her
pietade in sen.)   has no pity in his soul.)

CASSIO   CASSIO:
(L'ora è fatal! un fulmine sul mio   (It is a fatal hour! Lightning points out
cammin l'addita.   the dangers on my path.
Già di mia sorte il culmine s'offre   Already my fate surrenders to the
all'inerte incalza   dangers that pursue me.
L'ebbra fortuna incalza la fuga della   The intoxicated fortune pursues an
vita.   escaping life.
Questa che al ciel m'innalza è un'onda Heaven praises me with a wave of a
d'uragan.)   hurricane.)

RODERIGO:
(Per me s'oscura il mondo, s'annuvola
il destin, l'angol soave e biondo
scompar dal mio cammin.)

LODOVICO:
(Egli la man funerea scuote anelando
d'ira, essa la faccia eterea volge
piangendo al ciel.
Nel contemplar quel pianto la carità
sospira, e un tenero compianto
stempra del core il gel.)

DESDEMONA:
E un di sul mio sorriso
fioria la speme e il bacio,
ed or, l'angoscia in viso
e l'agonia nel cor.
A terra, nel fango, percossa, io giacio,
m'agghiaccia il brivido dell'anima che
muor.

DAME:
Pietà! Pietà! Pietà!
Ansia mortale, bieca, ne ingombra,
anime assorte in lungo orror.
Vista crudel!
Ei la colpi! Quel viso santo, pallido,
blando, si china e tace e piange e muor.
Piangon così nel ciel lor pianto gli
angeli quando perduto giace il peccator.

CAVALIERI:
Mistero! Mistero! Mistero!
Quell'uomo nero è sepolcrale, e cieca
un'ombra è in lui di morte e di terror!
Strazia coll'ugna l'orrido
petto! Gli sguardi figge immoti al suol.
Poi sfida il ciel coll'atre pugna, l'ispido
aspetto ergendo ai dardi alti del Sol.

RODERIGO:
(For me, the world darkens into a
clouded destiny, and the gentle blond
angel disappears from my path.)

LODOVICO:
(His bleak hand shakes and he gasps
with anger. She turns her delicate face
to Heaven and weeps.
In contemplating those tears, charity
sighs, and a tender sorrow melts the
chilled heart.

DESDEMONA:
And once my smile flourished with
hope and a kiss,
and now, there is anguish on my face
and agony in my heart.
On the ground,,, in the murky slime,
struck down, the shiver of my chills in
my dying soul.

WOMEN:
Mercy! Mercy! Mercy!
Fierce mortal anguish, thoughts of evil
have overcome his mind.
Cruel sight!
He struck her! That saintly face, pale and
gentle, says nothing and cries and dies.
The angels in heaven also cry when
they have lost the sinner.

MEN:
A mystery! A mystery! A mystery!
That dark man is deathlike, a blind
shadow of death and terror in him!
With clenched hands he wildly beats
his chest! He challenges the Heavens
with his other fist, raising his beastly
look to the sun's rays.

JAGO:
Una parola.

IAGO: *(approaching Othello)*
A word

OTELLO:
E che?

OTHELLO:
And what?

JAGO:
T'affretta! Rapido slancia la tua
vendetta! Il tempo vola.

IAGO:
Hurry! Quickly take your revenge!
Time flies.

OTELLO:
Ben parli.

OTHELLO:
Good advice.

JAGO:
È l'ira inutil ciancia. Scuotiti!
All'opra ergi tua mira! All'opra sola!
Io penso a Cassio. Ei le sue trame
espia.
L'infame anima ria l'averno inghiotte!

IAGO:
Useless anger is nonsense! Get hold of
yourself! Concentrate on your action!
Only on your action! I will handle
Cassio. I'll spy on him.
The infernal will swallow his infamous soul!

OTELLO:
Chi gliela svelle?

OTHELLO:
Who will tear it from him?

JAGO:
Io.

IAGO:
I.

OTELLO:
Tu?

OTHELLO:
You?

JAGO:
Giurai.

IAGO:
I swear to it.

OTELLO:
Tal sia.

OTHELLO:
So be it.

JAGO:
Tu avrai le sue novelle questa notte.

IAGO:
You will have the news about him this evening.

(ironically to Roderigo)
(I sogni tuoi saranno in mar domani
e tu sull'aspra terra.)

(You dreams will be at sea tomorrow,
and you shall be on dry land.

RODERIGO:
(Ahi triste!)

JAGO:
Ahi stolto! Stolto!
Se vuoi, tu puoi sperar; gli umani,
orsù! Cimenti afferra, e m'odi.

RODERIGO:
T'ascolta.

JAGO:
Col primo albor salpa il vascello.
Or Cassio è il Duce.
Eppur se avvien che a questi accada
sventura, allor qui resta Otello.

RODERIGO:
Lugubre luce d'atro balen!

JAGO:
Mano alla spada!
A notte folta io la sua traccia vigilo,
e il varco e l'ora scruto; il resto a te.
Sarò tuo scolta. A caccia! a caccia!
Cingiti l'arco!)

RODERIGO:
(Sì! T'ho venduto onore e fè.)

JAGO:
(Corri al miraggio! Il fragile tuo senno
ha già confuso un sogno menzogner.
Segui l'astuto ed agile mio cenno,
amante illuso, io seguo il mio pensier.)

RODERIGO:
(Il dado è tratto! Impavido t'attendo,
ultima sorte, occulto mio destin.
Mi sprona amor, ma un avido, tremendo
astro di morte infesta il mio cammin.)

RODERIGO:
(So sad!)

IAGO:
Foolish! Foolish!
If you wish, you can wait. The men
now! Attack danger and listen to me.

RODERIGO:
I listen to you.

IAGO:
The vessel will sail at daybreak.
Now Cassio is the leader.
And yet if he should meet with a
mishap, Othello will remain here.

RODERIGO:
Dismal light of another flash!

IAGO:
Unsheathe your sword!
At full night I will watch his steps
I'll tell you the hour and place.
I will be your scout! To the hunt! To the
hunt! Get the bow ready!

RODERIGO:
(Yes! I have sold you my honor and faith!)

IAGO:
(The mirage proceeds! Your fragile mind
has already become confused by a lying
dreamer. Follow my astute and agile sign,
deceived lover. I follow my thoughts.)

RODERIGO:
(I await you fearlessly, final fate and
obscure destiny. Love guides me, but
an avid, terrible star of death infests
my path.)

OTELLO:
Fuggite!

OTHELLO:
Flee from me!

TUTTI:
Ciel!

ALL:
Heavens!

OTELLO:
Tutti fuggite Otello!

OTHELLO:
Everyone flee from Othello!

JAGO:
Lo assale una malia che d'ogni senso il
priva.

IAGO: *(to all)*
He is stricken by an illness that
deprives him of all of his senses.

OTELLO:
Chi non si scosta è contro me rubello.

OTHELLO:
Who doesn't leave must face my whip.

Desdemona runs toward Othello.

LODOVICO:
Mi segui.

LODOVICO: *(trying to draw her away)*
Follow me.

CIPRIOTTI:
Evviva!

CYPRIOTS:
Hail!

DESDEMONA:
Mio sposo!

DESDEMONA:
My husband!

OTELLO:
Anima mia, ti maledico!

OTHELLO:
My dearest, I curse you!

TUTTI:
Orror!

ALL:
Horror!

All leave. Othello and Iago are alone.

OTELLO:
Fuggirmi io sol non so!
Sangue!
Ah! L'abbietto pensiero!
"Ciò m'accora!"
Vederli insieme avvinti.
Il fazzoletto! Il fazzoletto! Il fazzoletto!
Ah! Ah! Ah!

OTHELLO: *(delirious)*
I cannot flee from myself!
Blood!
Ah! That vile thought!
"This breaks my heart!"
To see them embraced together.
The handkerchief! The handkerchief!
The handkerchief! Ah! Ah! Ah!

JAGO:
(Il mio valen lavora.)

IAGO:
(My poison is working.)

CIPRIOTTI:
Viva Otello!

CYPRIOTS: *(from outside)*
Long live Othello!

JAGO:
L'eco della vittoria....

IAGO:
The echo of victory....

CIPRIOTTI:
Evviva, viva!

CYPRIOTS:
Hail, long life!

JAGO:
....porge sua laude estrema.

IAGO:
....gives him extreme praise.

CIPRIOTTI:
Evviva!

CYPRIOTS:
Hail!

Iago observes Othello lying on the ground

JAGO:
Chi può vietar che questa fronte prema
col mio tallone?

IAGO:
Who can prevent me from placing my
heel on his head?

CIPRIOTTI:
Evviva! Evviva Otello!
Gloria al Leon di Venezia!

CYPRIOTS:
Hail! Hail Othello!
Glory to the Lion of Venice!

JAGO:
Ecco il Leone!

IAGO: *(In irony and triumphant)*
Here is you Lion!

CIPRIOTTI:
Viva! Viva! Viva Otello!

CYPRIOTS:
Hail! Hail! Hail Othello!

ACT IV

Desdemona's bedroom.

EMILIA:
Era più calmo?

EMILIA:
He was calmer?

DESDEMONA:
Mi parea. M'ingiunse
di coricarmi e d'attenderlo.
Emilia, te ne prego, distendi sul mio
letto la mia candida veste nuziale.

Senti. Se pria di te morir dovessi
mi seppellisci con un di quei veli.

DESDEMONA:
It seemed so. He commanded me to go
to be and await him.
Emilia, I beg of you. Spread my white
wedding dress on my bed.

Listen. If I should die before you bury
me with one of those veils.

EMILIA:
Sacciate queste idee.

EMILIA:
Drive away those thoughts.

DESDEMONA:
Son mesta, tanto, tanto.

Mia madre aveva una povera ancella,
innamorata e bella. Era il suo nome
Barbara.
Amava un uom che poi l'abbandonò;
cantava un canzone: "La canzon del
Salice."

Mi disciogli le chiome.
Io questa sera ho la memoria piena
di quella cantilena.
"Piangea cantando nell'erma landa,
piangea la mesta.
O Salce! Salce! Salce!"

"Sedea chinando sul sen la testa!
Salce! Salce! Salce!
Cantiamo! Cantiamo! il Salce funebre
sarà la mia ghirlanda!"

DESDEMONA:
I'm so sad, so sad.

My mother had an old maidservant. She
was beautiful and in love. Her name
was Barbara.
The man she loved abandoned her; she
sang a song, "The Song of the
Willow."

Untie my hair.
This evening my thoughts are filled
with that song.
"Alone on the heath, she was sadly
weeping.
O Willow! Willow! Willow!"

"She sat with her head on her chest!
Willow! Willow! Willow!
Let's sing! Let's sing! The mournful
willow will be my garland!"

(to Emilia)

Affrettati; fra poco giunge Otello.   Hurry, soon Othello arrives.

DESDEMONA

"Scor-rea   -   no i ri   -   vi   fra le zolle in fior   gemea quel   core   affranto..."

"Scorreano i rivi fra le zolle in fior,   "The streams ran through the flowery
gemea quel core affranto,   banks. That broken heart was groaning,
e dalle ciglia le sgorgava il cor   and waves of bitter tears were gushing
l'amara onda del pianto.   from her eyes.
Salce! Salce! Salce!   Willow! Willow! Willow!
Cantiamo! Cantiamo! Il Salce funebre   Let's sing! Let's sing! The mournful
sarà la mia ghirlanda.   willow will be my garland.
Scendean 'angeli a vol dai rami cupi   All the birds descended from the
verso quel dolce canto.   branches to hear that sweet song.
E gli occhi suoi piangean tanto, tanto,   And her eyes were so full of tears that
da impietosir le rupi."   the stones were moved to pity."

(Desdemona takes a ring from her finger)

Riponi quest'anello.   Hold on to this ring.
Povera Barbara! Solea la storia con   Poor Barbara! That is how that sad
questo semplice suono finir: story ended.
"Egli era nato per la sua gloria,   "He was born for glory, and I for love."
io per amar."

Ascolta. Odo un lamento.   Listen. I hear a sigh.
Taci. Chi batte a quella porta?   Quiet. Who knocks on the door?

EMILIA: **EMILIA:**
E il vento.   It is the wind.

DESDEMONA: **DESDEMONA:**
"Io per amarlo e per morir.   "And I to love him and to die.
Cantiamo! Cantiamo!   Let's sing! Let's sing!
Salce! Salce! Salce!"   Willow! Willow! Willow!"

Emilia, addio. Come m'ardon le ciglia!   Farewell Emilia. How my eyes are
È presagio di pianto.   burning me! I feel like crying.
Buona notte.   Good night.
Ah! Emilia, Emilia, addio, Emilia, addio!   Ah! Emilia, Emilia, farewell!

Ave Maria, piena di grazia, eletta
fra le spose e le vergini sei tu,
sia benedetto il frutto, o benedetta,
di tue materne viscere, Gesù.

Hail Mary, full of grace, you the elite
among women and virgins,
and from your maternal womb, the
blessed fruit: Jesus.

Adagio
DESDEMONA

Pre - ga per chi a do-ran - do a   te,   si   pro - stra,

Prega per chi adorando a te si prostra,
prega nel peccator, per l'innocente,
e pel debole oppresso e pel possente,
misero anch'esso, tua pietà dimostra.

Pray for one who kneels before you and
adores you. Pray for the sinner, for the
innocent, and for the oppressed weak,
and also show mercy for the powerful.

Prega per chi sotto l'oltraggio piega
la fronte e sotto la malvagia sorte;
per noi, per noi tu prega, prega
sempre e nell'ora della morte nostra,
prega per noi, prega per noi, prega.

Pray for one who bows the head under
outrage and wicked destiny.
Pray for us. pray always, and at the
hour of our death, pray for us.
Pray for us, pray.

Ave Maria, nell'ora della morte.
Ave! Amen!

Hail Mary, in the hour of death.
Hail! Amen!

Desdemona lies down on the bed. Othello enters from a secret door.
With gestures of fury he approaches the bed and contemplates the sleeping
Desdemona. He kisses her, awakening her with the third kiss.

DESDEMONA:
Chi è là? Otello?

DESDEMONA:
Who is there? Othello?

OTELLO:
Sì! Diceste questa sera le vostre preci?

OTHELLO:
Yes! You said your prayers tonight?

DESDEMONA:
Orai. . .

DESDEMONA:
I prayed.

OTELLO:
Se vi sovviene di qualche colpa
commessa che attenda grazia dal ciel,
imploratela tosto.

OTHELLO:
Implore the grace of heaven if it helps
to absolve a crime you have committed
and which awaits grace.

DESDEMONA:
Perchè?

OTELLO:
T'affretta. Uccidere non voglio l'anima tua.

DESDEMONA:
D'uccider parli?

OTELLO:
Sì.

DESDEMONA:
Pietà di me, mio Dio!

OTELLO:
Amen.

DESDEMONA:
E abbiate pietà voi pure.

OTELLO:
Pensa ai tuoi peccati.

DESDEMONA:
Mio peccato è l'amor.

OTELLO:
Perciò tu muori.

DESDEMONA:
E perchè t'amo m'uccidi?

OTELLO:
Ami Cassio.

DESDEMONA:
No! Sull'anima mia!

OTELLO:
Quel fazzoletto ch'io ti donai gli desti.

DESDEMONA:
Why?

OTHELLO:
Hurry! I don't want to kill your soul.

DESDEMONA:
You speak of killing?

OTHELLO::
Yes.

DESDEMONA:
God have mercy on me!

OTHELLO:
Amen.

DESDEMONA:
And you too have mercy.

OTHELLO:
Think about your sins.

DESDEMONA:
My sin is love.

OTHELLO:
For that you die.

DESDEMONA:
And you kill me because I love you?

OTHELLO:
You love Cassio.

DESDEMONA:
No! On my soul!

OTHELLO:
You gave that handkerchief to him.

DESDEMONA:
Non è vero.

OTELLO:
Nella sua man lo vidi.

DESDEMONA:
Io rea non sono!

OTELLO:
Confessa!

DESDEMONA:
Giuro!

OTELLO:
Bada allo spergiuro.
Pensa che sei sul tuo letto di morte.

DESDEMONA:
Non per morir.

OTELLO:
Per morir tosto.

DESDEMONA:
Aita!
Cassio non amo, ch'ei qui venga, ei
parli.

OTELLO:
Muto è per sempre.

DESDEMONA:
Cielo! Morto?

OTELLO:
Morto.

DESDEMONA:
Son perduta! Ei tradito!

DESDEMONA:
That's not true.

OTHELLO:
I saw it in his hand.

DESDEMONA:
I am not guilty!

OTHELLO:
Confess!

DESDEMONA:
I swear!

OTHELLO:
Stop your lying.
Think that you are on your deathbed.

DESDEMONA:
Not to die.

OTHELLO:
To die right now.

DESDEMONA:
Help me!
I don't love Cassio. Call him here and
ask him.

OTHELLO:
He is silent for ever.

DESDEMONA:
Heavens! Dead?

OTHELLO:
Dead.

DESDEMONA:
I am lost and betrayed!

OTELLO:
E pianger l'osi?

DESDEMONA:
Otello, non uccidermi.

OTELLO:
Tu invano ti difendi.

DESDEMONA:
Ch'io viva ancor, ch'io viva ancor,
ch'io viva ancor.

OTELLO:
Giù! Cadi, giù, cadi, prostituta.

DESDEMONA:
Pietà!

OTELLO:
Muori!

DESDEMONA:
Ch'io viva questa notte.

OTELLO:
No!

DESDEMONA:
Un'ora.

OTELLO:
No!

DESDEMONA:
Un istante.

OTELLO:
No!

DESDEMONA:
Sol ch'io dica un'Ave.

OTHELLO:
And you dare cry for him?

DESDEMONA:
Othello, don't kill me.

OTHELLO:
It is futile to defend yourself.

DESDEMONA:
That I may live, that I may live,
that I may live.

OTHELLO:
Down! Fall down, down, prostitute.

DESDEMONA:
Mercy!

OTHELLO:
Die!

DESDEMONA:
Let me live just tonight.

OTHELLO:
No!

DESDEMONA:
For one hour.

OTHELLO:
No!

DESDEMONA:
For a moment.

OTHELLO:
No!

DESDEMONA:
If only that I can say a prayer.

OTELLO:
È tardi!

DESDEMONA:
Ah!. . .

OTELLO: :

Calma come la tomba.

EMILIA:
Aprite! Aprite!

OTELLO:
Chi è là? Chi batte?

EMILIA:
Signor mio, ven prego, lasciate
ch'io vi parli. Aprite!

OTELLO:
Emilia! Che avvenne?

EMILIA:
Un gran delitto! Cassio uccise Roderigo.

OTELLO:
E Cassio?

EMILIA:
Vive.

OTELLO:
Cassio vive!

DESDEMONA:
Ingiustamente, uccisa ingiustamente..

EMILIA:
Chi geme là? Orror!

OTHELLO:
It is too late!

(Othello suffocates Desdemona)
DESDEMONA:
Ah!

(Emilia knocks at the door)

OTHELLO:
(Contemplating the body of Desdemona)
Calm like the tomb.

EMILIA:
Open! Open!

OTHELLO:
Who is it? Who knocks?

EMILIA:
My lord. Hear me. Le me speak to you.
Open!

OTHELLO:
Emilia! What happened?

EMILIA:
A great crime! Cassio killed Roderigo.

OTHELLO:
And Cassio?

EMILIA:
He lives.

OTHELLO:
Cassio lives!

DESDEMONA:
Unjustly. I have been killed unjustly.

EMILIA:
Who is groaning there? Horror!

DESDEMONA:
Muoio innocente.

DESDEMONA:
I die innocent.

EMILIA:
Gran Dio! Chi fu? Chi fu?

EMILIA:
Oh God! Who did it? Who did it?

DESDEMONA:
Nessuno. Io stessa.
Al mio Signor mi raccomanda.
Muoio innocente.
Addio.

DESDEMONA:
No one. I myself.
I implore my soul to God.
I die guiltless.
Farewell.
(Desdemona dies)

OTELLO:
O mentitrice! Io l'uccisi.

OTHELLO:
Oh liar! I killed her.

EMILIA:
Assassino!

EMILIA:
Assassin!

OTELLO:
Fu di Cassio la druda. A Jago il chiedi.

OTHELLO:
She was Cassio's lover. Iago told me.

EMILIA:
A Jago?

EMILIA:
Iago?

OTELLO:
A Jago.

OTHELLO:
Iago.

EMILIA:
Stolto!! E tu il credesti?

EMILIA:
Fool! And you believed him?

OTELLO:
Negarlo ardisci?

OTHELLO:
You dare to deny it?

EMILIA:
Non ti temo.

EMILIA:
I have no fear of you.

OTELLO:
Bada!

OTHELLO:
Mind yourself!

EMILIA:
Olà! Soccorso! Aiuto!
Otello uccise Desdemona!

EMILIA:
Hello! Help! Rescue!
Othello killed Desdemona!

CASSIO, JAGO, LODOVICO:
Quai grida!
Orrore! Orror!

(Lodovico, Cassio and Iago enter)
CASSIO, IAGO, LODOVICO:
Who shouts! *(seeing Desdemona)*
Horror! Horror!

EMILIA:
Jago, smentisci quel vile assassino.
Hai tu creduto Desdemona infida?
Parla!

EMILIA: *(to Iago)*
Iago, refute that assassin.
Did you believe that Desdemona was
unfaithful? Speak!

JAGO:
Tal la credea.

IAGO:
I believed she was.

OTELLO:
Quel fazzoletto che un di le diedi,
a Cassio essa donava.

OTHELLO:
That handkerchief I once gave her, she
gave to Cassio.

EMILIA:
O potenza divina!

EMILIA:
Oh heavenly power!

JAGO:
Taci!

IAGO: *(to Emilia)*
Quiet!

EMILIA:
No, tutto rivelo!

EMILIA:
No, I will reveal all!

JAGO:
Taci!

IAGO:
Quiet!

EMILIA:
No! Costui dalla mia man quel
fazzoletto svelse a viva forza.

EMILIA:
No! He took that handkerchief from my
hand using force.

CASSIO:
E nella mia dimora trovai quel vel.

CASSIO:
And I found the veil in my room.

MONTANO:
Roderigo morente mi svelò di
quest'uom l'arti nefande.

MONTANO: *(enters and points to Iago)*
The dying Roderigo confessed this
man's nefarious plot.

OTELLO:
Ah! Discolpati!

OTHELLO: *(to Iago)*
Ah! Exculpate yourself!

JAGO:
No!

IAGO: *(flees)*
No!

LODOVICO:
Ferma!

LODOVICO:
Stop him!

MONTANO:
S'insegua.

MONTANO:
Follow him.

CASSIO, LODOVICO:
Afferratelo!

CASSIO, LODOVICO:
Don't let him escape!

OTELLO:
E il ciel non ha più fulmini?

OTHELLO: *(grabs his dagger)*
And does heaven have lightning left?

LODOVICO:
La spada a me!

LODOVICO:
Give me a sword!

OTELLO:
Tant'osi?

OTHELLO:
Just dare to?

OTELLO

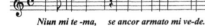

Niun mi te -ma,   se ancor armato mi ve-de.   *Ec - co la fi - ne del mio cammin.*

Niun mi tema s'anco armato mi vede.

No one fears me although they see me with a weapon.

Ecco la fine del mio camin.
Oh! Gloria! Otello fu.

This is the end of my road.
Oh! Glory! That was Othello.

Othello goes toward the bed, and contemplates Desdemona.

E tu. Come sei pallida! e stanca, e
muta, e bella,
pia creatura nata sotto maligna stella.
Fredda come la casta tua vita, .
e in cielo assorta.
Desdemona! Desdemona!
Ah, morta! morta! morta!

And you. How pale you are! And tired,
and silent, and beautiful, a pious
creature born under an evil star.
Cold like your chaste life,
and absorbed by the Heavens.
Desdemona! Desdemona!
Ah dead! Dead! Dead!

Ho un'arma ancor!

I yet have a weapon!
(Othello stabs himself)

CASSIO:
Ah! Ferma!

CASSIO:
Ah! Stop him!

LODOVICO, MONTANO:
Sciagurato!

LODOVICO, MONTANO:
Wicked man!

OTELLO:
Pria d'ucciderti, sposa, ti baciai.
Or morendo nell'ombra in cui mi giacio.
Un bacio, un bacio ancora.
Ah! Un altro bacio.

OTHELLO: *(to the dead Desdemona)*
Before I killed you, wife, I kissed you.
now dying in the shadow where I lie.
A kiss. Another kiss.
Ah! Another kiss.
(Othello dies)

Fine dell'Opera

END

Made in the USA
Monee, IL
25 January 2020